The Ultimate Guide to Twitter Income

Proven Strategies to Earn Money from Twitter: Steps to Build Your Twitter Account, Gain and Maintain Required Followers, and Impressions.

Isidore Bruno

Table of Content

Recover from Setbacks and Failures.

Chapter Seven

Innovative Tips for Success.

Experimenting and testing new features, formats, and strategies to optimize your Twitter income.

Leveraging tools and resources that can help you automate, streamline, and enhance your Twitter income activities.

Tips and best practices for choosing and using the right tools and resources.

Collaborating and networking with other Twitter users, influencers, and experts to learn, exchange, and support each other.

Diversifying and expanding your income streams and sources to increase your earning potential and reduce your risks.

Tips and steps for diversifying and expanding your income streams and sources.

Setting and tracking your goals and milestones and celebrating your achievements.

Continuously learning and improving your skills and knowledge in Twitter income generation.

Conclusion

Introduction

The Ultimate Guide to Twitter Income.

Discover how to make money from Twitter, the global social media giant with more than 330 million active users and 500 million daily tweets. It is also a powerful tool for generating income, whether you are an individual or a business, as it allows you to connect with your audience, promote your brand, drive traffic to your website, and monetize your content.

This book is designed to help you leverage the potential of Twitter and turn it into a profitable source of income. Whether you are a beginner or an expert, you will find valuable tips, tricks, and strategies to optimize your Twitter presence and achieve your income goals.

This book will benefit you if you belong to any of these categories:

Social Media Enthusiast and Influencer who is passionate about social media and is looking to maximize your income, particularly through platforms like Twitter. You will learn how to grow your followers, engage your audience, create viral content, and monetize your influence through various methods such as sponsored posts, affiliate marketing, product reviews, and more.

Entrepreneur or Business Owner seeking effective strategies to leverage Twitter for marketing and revenue generation. You will learn how to establish your brand identity, reach your target market, generate leads, increase conversions, and boost sales through Twitter. You will also discover how to use Twitter ads, analytics, and tools to enhance your marketing campaigns and measure your results.

Blogger and you want to drive more traffic to your websites and increase your ad revenue or affiliate income through Twitter. You will learn how to optimize your blog for Twitter, engagingly share your content, attract more visitors, and increase your click-through rates. You will also learn how to use hashtags, keywords, and trends to boost your visibility and reach on Twitter.

Freelancer and you want to showcase your skills and portfolio and attract more clients through Twitter. You will learn how to create a professional profile, network with potential clients, showcase your work, and pitch your services through Twitter. You will also learn how to use Twitter to find freelance opportunities, negotiate your rates, and manage your projects.

Author and you who want to build your personal brand and fan base and sell more books through Twitter. You will learn how to create a compelling author bio, interact with your readers, share your writing process, and promote your books through Twitter. You will also learn how to use Twitter to get feedback, reviews, and testimonials, and to collaborate with other authors and publishers.

Marketing and Digital Strategy Professional and you want to stay updated on the latest techniques and tactics for utilizing Twitter for business purposes. You will learn how to plan, implement, and evaluate your Twitter marketing strategy, and how to use best practices and industry standards to optimize your performance. You will also learn how to use Twitter to conduct market research, monitor your competitors, and identify new opportunities and trends.

Aspiring Social Media Manager and you want to enhance your skills and knowledge in optimizing Twitter for income generation. You will learn how to manage multiple Twitter accounts, create and schedule content, engage and moderate your community, and report and analyze your results. You will also learn how to use Twitter to provide customer service, handle crises, and build trust and loyalty.

If any of the descriptions mentioned above apply to you, then you are in the right place. Please continue reading to discover how you can turn Twitter into your ultimate income generator.

If you are not in any of the above categories, you may still benefit from this book if you have ever wondered:

How can I make money from Twitter?
How can I increase my followers and engagement on Twitter?
How can I create content that stands out and attracts attention on Twitter?
How can I use Twitter to market my products or services?
How can I use Twitter to grow my brand or business?
How can I use Twitter to improve my skills and career prospects?

If you have ever asked yourself any of these questions, then this book is for you. Please continue reading to find the answers and more.

This twitter guide will cover a variety of topics, including:
Strategic Account Building: How to create a captivating profile, optimize your bio, and choose a niche that suits your passion and expertise. You will learn how to craft a catchy username, a memorable profile picture, a compelling header image, and a clear and concise bio that showcases your value proposition and personality. You will also learn how to identify and target your

ideal audience, and how to choose a niche that aligns with your passion, expertise, and goals.

Follower Acquisition and Retention Tactics: How to attract and retain loyal followers who are interested in your content and willing to engage with you. You will learn how to create and share valuable, relevant, and engaging content that resonates with your audience and showcases your authority and credibility. You will also learn how to interact with your followers and other users, how to join and start conversations, how to use mentions, retweets, likes, and comments effectively, and how to encourage user-generated content and feedback.

Optimizing Impressions: How to boost your impressions, reach, and visibility by using hashtags, keywords, and trending topics effectively. You will learn how to research and use hashtags that are relevant to your niche, your content, and your audience. You will also learn how to optimize your keywords and phrases for search engine optimization (SEO) and discoverability. Moreover, you will learn how to leverage trending topics and events to create timely and topical content that attracts attention and engagement.

Proven Income Strategies: How to leverage different methods of making money from Twitter, such as sponsored tweets, selling products and services, affiliate marketing, creator subscriptions, ads revenue sharing, and more. You will learn how to monetize your Twitter account by partnering with brands and businesses that are aligned with your niche and audience, and how to create and post sponsored tweets that are authentic and effective. You will also learn how to sell your own products and services, such as e-books, courses, coaching, consulting, etc., and how to drive traffic and conversions from Twitter to your website or landing page. Furthermore, you will learn how to become an affiliate marketer and promote other people's products and services, and how to earn commissions from every sale you generate. Additionally, you will learn how to launch creator subscriptions and offer exclusive content and perks to your loyal fans and supporters, and how to join the X Ads Revenue Sharing Program and earn money from the ads that are shown on your tweets.

Avoid Common Mistakes: How to avoid pitfalls and challenges that can hinder your Twitter income, such as spamming, violating rules, losing followers, and more. You will learn how to avoid spamming your followers and other users with excessive and irrelevant tweets, links, and hashtags, and how to follow the Twitter rules and guidelines to avoid getting suspended or banned. You will also learn how to avoid losing followers and engagement by maintaining a consistent and high-quality content schedule, and by avoiding controversial, offensive, or negative topics and comments.

Innovative Tips for Success: Stay ahead of the curve with cutting-edge tips and tricks to navigate the ever-evolving landscape of Twitter income generation. You will learn how to use analytics and insights to measure and improve your performance, and how to test and optimize different strategies and tactics. You will also learn how to use tools and resources to automate and streamline your Twitter activities, and how to stay updated and informed on the latest trends and developments in the Twitter world.

Get started and increase your income, create an ecosystem for your brand and promote it, improve your media visibility, and many more...

This book is more than just a guide. It's a blueprint for success. It will show you how to use Twitter to your advantage, and how to turn your passion and expertise into a profitable and sustainable online business. Whether you are a beginner or an expert, a hobbyist or a professional, a creator or a marketer, this book will help you achieve your goals and dreams.

Don't miss this opportunity to join the millions of people who are making money from Twitter. Read this book to the end and start your journey to Twitter income. You won't regret it.

Chapter One

Strategic Account Building.

Twitter is a powerful platform for sharing ideas, creating trends, and building connections. Millions of people use Twitter every day to communicate, learn, and entertain themselves. But there is more to Twitter than just socializing and having fun. You can also turn it into a profitable online business.

Yes, you read that right. Twitter is not only a social media network, but also a potential source of income for anyone who knows how to use it effectively. Whether you want to sell your products or services, promote your brand or business, or monetize your content or influence, Twitter can help you achieve your goals and dreams.

But before you can start earning money from Twitter, you need to take the first and most important step: building a strategic and attractive Twitter account.

Welcome to Chapter 1 of The Ultimate Guide to Twitter Income, where we will guide you through the process of creating and optimizing your Twitter account for success. In this chapter, you will learn the essential elements of a high-quality Twitter account that will help you stand out from the crowd, attract and retain loyal followers, and establish your credibility and authority in your niche and industry.

Your Twitter account is the foundation of your Twitter income strategy. It is your online identity, your digital storefront, and your billboard. It is where you showcase your brand, personality, and value proposition to the world. It is where you connect with your audience, engage with your peers, and influence your industry. It is where you create and share valuable content that educates, entertains, and inspires your followers.

Therefore, you need to make sure that your Twitter account is professional, appealing, and effective. You need to make sure that your Twitter account reflects who you are, what you do, and why you matter. You need to make sure that your Twitter account is strategically designed to achieve your goals and objectives.

In this chapter, we will show you how to do that. We will cover the following topics:

How to choose a username and display name that reflects your brand and personality, and makes you easy to find and remember.
How to write a catchy and informative bio that showcases your value proposition and credibility, and encourages people to follow you and check out your website or other links.
How to select a profile picture and header image that attracts attention conveys your message, and matches your brand identity and aesthetics.
How to find and follow relevant accounts in your niche and industry, and build relationships with potential customers, partners, and mentors.
How to define your target audience and their needs and preferences, and tailor your content and communication to them.
How to develop your unique voice and style that resonates with your followers, and reflects your personality and values.

By the end of this chapter, you will have a complete and compelling Twitter account that sets you apart from the competition and positions you as an expert and influencer in your field. This will enable you to leverage the power of Twitter to generate income and grow your online business.

Are you ready to start building your strategic Twitter account? Let's get started!

Choosing a Username and Display Name.

Your username and display name are the first things that people see when they encounter your Twitter account. They are also the main identifiers that people use to find and follow you on the platform. Therefore, choosing a username and display name that reflects your brand and personality is crucial for creating a memorable and consistent Twitter identity.

Choose a username that is unique, relevant, and easy to remember: Your username is the handle that appears after the @ symbol on your profile and tweets. It can be up to 15 characters long and can contain letters, numbers, and underscores. Your username is also the primary way that people can search for you and mention you on Twitter.

When choosing a username, you should consider the following factors:

Uniqueness: Your username should be distinctive and not easily confused with other accounts. Avoid using generic or common words, such as John, Jane, or Twitter. Instead, try to incorporate your name, initials, nickname, or something that represents you or your brand.

Relevance: Your username should be relevant to your purpose and audience on Twitter. For example, if you are a professional, you may want to use your full name or a variation of it, such as @JohnSmith or @JSmith. If you are a business, you may want to use your company name or a shortened version of it, such as @Microsoft or @MSFT. If you are creative, you may want to use your stage name or a catchy phrase that describes your work, such as @LadyGaga or @TheWeeknd.

Memorability: Your username should be easy to remember and spell for your followers and potential followers. Avoid using numbers or symbols that are hard to type or pronounce, such as @4ever21 or @$tarbucks. Instead, use words or abbreviations that are familiar and meaningful, such as @Nike or @BBC.

Avoid common username mistakes that can hurt your brand and credibility: Choosing a username that is unique, relevant, and easy to remember is not enough to ensure a successful Twitter identity. You should also avoid some common username mistakes that can hurt your brand and credibility, such as:

Changing your username frequently: Changing your username can confuse your followers and make it harder for them to find you and interact with you. It can also affect your search ranking and visibility on Twitter. Therefore, you should choose a username that you are happy with and stick with it as long as possible. If you do need to change your username, you should inform your followers beforehand and redirect them to your new account.

Using a username that is offensive, misleading, or impersonating: Using a username that is offensive, misleading, or impersonating can damage your reputation and trustworthiness on Twitter. It can also violate Twitter's rules and policies and result in your account being suspended or banned. Therefore, you should choose a username that is respectful, honest, and authentic. You should also avoid using a username that is similar to or copies another account, especially if it is a verified or well-known account.

Using a username that is unrelated to your display name: Using a username that is unrelated to your display name can create confusion and inconsistency for your followers and potential followers. It can also make it harder for them to recognize you and remember you. Therefore, you should choose a username that is closely related to or matches your display name. For example, if your display name is John Smith, you can use a username such as @JohnSmith, @JSmith, or @John_Smith.

Use keywords, and abbreviations to make your username stand out: If you want to make your username stand out from the crowd and attract more attention and followers, you can use some creative techniques, such as:

Using keywords: Keywords are words or phrases that describe your niche, industry, or topic of interest. By using keywords in your username, you can showcase your expertise and relevance and increase your chances of being found by people who are looking for your content. For example, if you are a fitness trainer, you can use a username such as @FitCoach or @FitnessTips. If you are a travel blogger, you can use a username such as @TravelWithMe or @Wanderlust.

Using abbreviations: Abbreviations are shortened forms of words or phrases that are commonly used or recognized. By using abbreviations in your username, you can save space and make your username more catchy and memorable. For example, if you are a fan of the Harry Potter series, you can use a username such as @HPFan or @Potterhead. If you are a fan of the Marvel Cinematic Universe, you can use a username such as @MCUFan or @MarvelLover.

Choose a display name that complements your username and conveys your message: Your display name is the name that appears on your profile and tweets, above your username. It can be up to 50 characters long and can contain any characters, including spaces, emojis, and punctuation. Your display name is also the name that people see when they receive notifications from you or when they reply to your tweets.

When choosing a display name, you should consider the following factors:

Complementarity: Your display name should complement your username and create a cohesive and consistent Twitter identity. For example, if your username is @JohnSmith, your display name can be John Smith, John, Smith, or something that relates to your username, such as John the Writer or Smith the Lawyer.

Message: Your display name should convey your message and purpose on Twitter. For example, if you are a professional, you may want to use your full name or a variation of it, such as John Smith or J. Smith, to establish your credibility and authority. If you are a business, you may want to use your company name or a variation of it, such as Microsoft or MSFT, to promote your brand and products. If you are an artiste, you may want to use your stage name or a catchy phrase that describes your work, such as Lady Gaga or The Weeknd.

Use capitalization, and punctuation to enhance your display name: If you want to enhance your display name and make it more appealing and expressive, you can use some creative techniques, such as:

Using capitalization: Capitalization is the use of uppercase and lowercase letters to emphasize or distinguish certain words or letters. By using capitalization in your display name, you can create contrast and highlight your message and personality. For example, if you want to show your enthusiasm and excitement, you can use a display name such as JOHN SMITH or John SMITH. If you want to show your creativity and uniqueness, you can use a display name such as jOhN sMiTh or JoHn SmItH.

Using punctuation: Punctuation is the use of marks or signs to separate or clarify sentences, words, or parts of words. By using punctuation in your display name, you can add some style and flair to your display name and make it more catchy and memorable. For example, if you want to add some humor and fun to your display name, you can use a display name such as John Smith?. If you want to add some drama and suspense to your display name, you can use a display name such as John Smith... or John Smith!.

Writing a Catchy and Informative Bio.

Your bio is the second thing that people see when they visit your Twitter profile, after your profile picture. It is also the main source of information that people use to decide whether to follow you or not. Therefore, writing a catchy and informative bio that showcases your value proposition and credibility is essential for attracting and retaining loyal followers.

Write a bio that summarizes who you are, what you do, and why people should follow you:

The first step to writing a good bio is to introduce yourself to your potential followers. You want to give them a clear idea of who you are, what you do, and why they should care. You can achieve this by asking yourself three questions:

Who are you? This is where you state your name, your role, your company, or any other relevant information that defines your identity.
What do you do? This is where you describe what you offer, what you specialize in, what you are passionate about, or what you are working on.
Why should people follow you? This is where you highlight your value proposition, your unique selling point, your credibility, or your purpose.

For example, here is a bio that answers these three questions:

I'm John Smith, a freelance writer and editor. I help businesses create engaging and persuasive content that drives traffic and conversions. Follow me for tips, insights, and opportunities in the content marketing industry.

Notice how this bio tells the reader who John is, what he does, and why they should follow him. It also uses keywords like **freelance writer**, **editor**, and **content marketing** which can help him rank higher in Twitter search results.

Use keywords, hashtags, and links to optimize your bio for search and discovery:

One of the benefits of having a catchy and informative bio is that it can help you get discovered by more people who are interested in your niche, your industry, or your topic. To optimize your bio for search and discovery, you need to use keywords, hashtags, and links strategically.

Keywords are words or phrases that describe your topic, your niche, your industry, or your expertise. They can help you appear in relevant search results and attract more followers who are looking for what you offer. For example, if you are a fitness coach, you can use keywords like **fitness**, **health**, **wellness**, **workout**, or **nutrition** in your bio.

Hashtags are words or phrases that start with a # symbol and are used to categorize tweets by topic. They can help you join trending conversations, reach new audiences, and show your involvement in your community. For example, if you are a fitness coach, you can use hashtags like **#FitnessFriday**, **#WorkoutWednesday**, or **#HealthyLifestyle** in your bio.

Links are URLs that direct people to your website, your blog, your portfolio, your landing page, or any other online resource that you want to promote. They can help you drive more traffic, generate more leads, and showcase your work. For example, if you are a fitness coach, you can use a link to your website, your blog, or your online course in your bio.

Here is an example of a bio that uses keywords, hashtags, and links effectively:

I'm Jane Doe, a nutritionist and fitness coach with a certification. I provide online coaching customized to your health and fitness objectives. Follow me for #FitnessFriday suggestions and explore my website for more tools. janedoe.com

Notice how this bio uses keywords like fitness coach, nutritionist, and online coaching to describe what Jane does and what she offers. It also uses a hashtag like #FitnessFriday to join a popular conversation and a link to her website to drive more traffic.

Use humor, personality, and storytelling to make your bio engaging and authentic:

Another way to make your bio catchy and informative is to use humor, personality, and storytelling to make it engaging and authentic. You want to show your human side, your voice, and your style to your followers. You want to make them laugh, smile, or relate to you. You want to make them feel like they know you, like you, and trust you.

Humor is the use of jokes, sarcasm, irony, or wit to make your bio funny, clever, or amusing. It can help you stand out from the crowd, show your sense of humor, and make your followers smile. **For example, here is a bio that uses humor:**

I'm Bob Jones, a professional procrastinator and occasional blogger. I write about things that interest me, mostly Netflix and pizza. Follow me for mediocre content and bad jokes.

Personality is the use of words, emojis, or punctuation to show your tone, your mood, or your attitude. It can help you express yourself, show your emotions, and make your followers feel closer to you.
For example, here is a bio that uses personality:

I'm Alice Lee, a digital nomad and travel blogger. Exploring new places, meeting new people, and learning new things are my passions. Follow me for amazing photos, stories, and tips from around the world.

Storytelling is the use of anecdotes, facts, or details to tell a story about yourself, your brand, or your mission. It can help you create a narrative, share your background, and interest your followers.
For example, here is a bio that uses storytelling:

I'm Charlie Brown, a former lawyer turned chocolate maker. I quit my corporate job to pursue my passion for making delicious and ethical chocolate. Follow me for behind-the-scenes glimpses of my chocolate factory and my journey as an entrepreneur.

Update your bio regularly to reflect your current goals and achievements:

Your bio is not a static piece of text that you write once and forget. It is a dynamic and flexible tool that you can use to showcase your current goals and achievements. You can update your bio regularly to reflect your latest projects, your recent accomplishments, or your current challenges. This can help you keep your followers updated, interested, and engaged.

You can change your bio to something like this:
Announce a new product, a new service, a new book, or a new course that you have launched or are working on.
Share a milestone, an award, a recognition, or a testimonial that you have achieved or received
Promote an event, a webinar, a podcast, or a live session that you are hosting or participating in.
Highlight a cause, campaign, charity, or movement you are supporting or advocating for.
Change your location, your role, your company, or your status if you have moved, switched jobs, or made any significant changes in your life or career.

Here are some examples of how you can update your bio to reflect your current goals and achievements:

I'm John Smith, a freelance writer and editor. I help businesses create engaging and persuasive content that drives traffic and conversions. Follow me for tips, insights, and opportunities in the content marketing industry. Excited to announce that I'm working on my first book, coming soon!

I'm Jane Doe, a certified fitness coach and nutritionist. I help busy professionals achieve their health and fitness goals with personalized online coaching. Follow me for #FitnessFriday tips and check out my website for more resources. Honored to be featured in the Top 10 Fitness Coaches of 2023 by Fitness Magazine

I'm Bob Jones, a professional procrastinator and occasional blogger. I write about things that interest me, mostly Netflix and pizza. Follow me for mediocre content and bad jokes. Join me for a live Q&A session on how to overcome procrastination on Tuesday at 3 pm EST.

Use pinned tweets, highlights, and fleets to supplement your bio with additional information:

Your bio is not the only place where you can share information about yourself or your brand. You can also use pinned tweets, highlights, and fleets to supplement your bio with additional information that can help you attract and retain more followers.

Pinned tweets are tweets that you can pin to the top of your profile so that they are always visible to your visitors. You can use pinned tweets to:
Showcase your best work, your most popular content, or your most valuable offer.
Provide a call to action, a link, or contact information that you want your followers to take.
Introduce yourself, your brand, or your mission in a more personal or detailed way.

To pin a tweet, you need to follow these steps:
Go to Twitter app or website and log in to your account.
Navigate to your profile page and locate the tweet you want to pin.
Tap or click the three-dot menu icon at the top-right corner of the tweet.
Choose **Pin to your profile** from the menu options.
Confirm your choice by tapping or clicking **Pin**.

That's it! Your tweet will now be pinned to your profile and will appear above your other tweets. You can only have one pinned tweet at a time, so if you want to change it, you need to unpin the current one and pin a new one. You can also unpin a tweet anytime by following the same steps and selecting **Unpin from profile** instead.

Highlights are collections of tweets that you can group by topic, theme, or category. You can use highlights to:
Organize your tweets by different aspects of your niche, your industry, or your expertise.
Curate your tweets with different types of content, such as articles, videos, podcasts, or infographics.
Showcase your tweets by different events, such as conferences, webinars, interviews, or collaborations.

To use highlight on your Twitter bio, you need to follow these steps:

Go to the Twitter app or website and log in to your account.
Navigate to your profile page and tap or click the **Edit profile** button.
Tap or click the **Add highlight** button below your bio.
Choose the type of highlight you want to create: tweets, moments, or lists.
Select the tweets, moments, or lists you want to include in your highlight. You can add up to five items per highlight.
Give your highlight a name and a description. You can also choose a cover image from the items you selected or upload your own.
Tap or click the **Save** button to create your highlight.

That's it! Your highlight will now be displayed on your profile page below your bio. You can edit, reorder, or delete your highlights anytime by tapping or clicking the **Edit profile** button again.

Fleets are short-lived stories that disappear after 24 hours. You can use fleets to:
Share behind-the-scenes glimpses, sneak peeks, or teasers of your work, your projects, or your life.
Engage with your followers, ask questions, get feedback, or start conversations.

To create a Fleet, follow these steps:

Tap your profile image on the Timeline tab.
Choose the type of Fleet you want to create: text, photo, video, or tweet.
Customize your Fleet with background colors, text options, stickers, or emojis.
Tap the Fleet button to post your Fleet.

Your Fleet will appear on your profile page below your bio and at the top of your followers' home timeline. You can see who viewed your Fleet by tapping on it and looking at the **Seen By**' text at the bottom. You can also edit, reorder, or delete your Fleets anytime by tapping the **Edit profile** button on your profile page.

Here are some examples of how you can use pinned tweets, highlights, and fleets to supplement your bio with additional information:

Pinned tweet: I'm so excited to share with you my new online course on how to write catchy and informative bios for Twitter. Learn the best practices, tips, and tricks from a professional writer and editor. Enroll now and get a 50% discount with this link.

Highlight: Writing Tips. A collection of tweets where I share my best writing tips, such as how to write catchy headlines, how to avoid common grammar mistakes, and how to edit your work.

Fleet: Hey everyone, I'm working on a new blog post about how to optimize your bio for search and discovery. What are some of the keywords, hashtags, or links that you use in your bio? I would love to hear from you in the comments or a private message.

By following these steps, you can create a bio that showcases your value proposition, your credibility, and your personality. You can also use your bio as a tool to promote your work, your brand, or your mission. Remember, your bio is the first impression that you make on your potential followers, so make it count.

Selecting a Profile Picture and Header Image.

Your profile picture and header image are among the first things that people see when they land on your Twitter profile. They are also the main visual elements that people use to form an impression of you and your brand. Therefore, selecting a profile picture and header image that attracts attention and conveys your message is vital for creating a professional and appealing Twitter presence.

Pick a photo that shows who you are and what you do:

Your profile picture is the small circular image that appears next to your name and username on your profile and tweets. It is one of the first things that people notice when they visit your profile or see your tweets. Your profile picture should represent you and your brand in a way that is consistent, recognizable, and authentic.

If you are using Twitter for personal purposes, such as sharing your opinions, interests, or hobbies, you should use a photo of yourself as your profile picture. This will help people to connect with you as a person and to trust your voice. If you are using Twitter for professional or business purposes, such as promoting your products, services, or expertise, you should use a logo or a photo of yourself that reflects your brand identity and values. This will help people to recognize your brand and to associate it with your message.

Some tips for choosing a profile picture that represents you and your brand are:

Use a photo that shows your face clearly and that is appropriate for your audience and purpose. Avoid using photos that are blurry, dark, or cropped too tightly or loosely. Also, avoid using photos that are too casual, formal, or provocative, unless they match your brand personality and tone.

Use a recent photo that reflects your current appearance and style. Avoid using photos that are outdated, misleading, or irrelevant. For example, do not use a photo of yourself from 10 years ago, a photo of yourself wearing a hat or sunglasses that obscures your face or a photo of yourself in a different context or location that has nothing to do with your brand or message.

Use a photo that expresses your personality and mood. Avoid using photos that are bland, boring, or generic. Instead, use photos that show your emotions, passions, or interests. For example, you can use a photo of yourself smiling, laughing, or making a funny face or a photo of yourself doing something you love, such as playing an instrument, reading a book, or traveling.

Use a photo that matches your color scheme and theme. Avoid using photos that clash with your profile design or that are too busy or distracting. Instead, use photos that complement your profile colors and that have a simple and clean background. For example, you can use a photo of yourself wearing a shirt or a scarf that matches your profile color, or a photo of yourself in front of a plain wall or a natural scenery.

Use a high-quality, clear, and recent photo of yourself or your logo:

Once you have chosen a photo of yourself or your logo that represents you and your brand, you need to make sure that it is high-quality, clear, and recent. A high-quality, clear, and recent photo will make your profile look more professional, credible, and attractive. A low-quality, blurry, or outdated photo will make your profile look amateurish, untrustworthy, and unappealing.

Some tips for using a high-quality, clear, and recent photo of yourself or your logo are:

Use a photo that has a resolution of at least 400 x 400 pixels. This will ensure that your profile picture looks sharp and crisp on any device or screen size. Avoid using photos that are too small, pixelated, or stretched. Also, avoid using photos that are too large, as they may take longer to load or be cropped by Twitter.

Use a photo that has a good contrast and brightness. This will ensure that your profile picture stands out and is visible on any background or theme. Avoid using photos that are too dark, light, or faded. Also, avoid using photos that have too many colors, patterns, or effects, as they may look messy or confusing.

Use a photo that is current and accurate. This will ensure that your profile picture reflects your present situation and status. Avoid using photos that are old, outdated, or irrelevant. For example, do not use a photo of yourself from a previous job or role, or a photo of your logo from a previous version or design.

Use filters, frames, and stickers to enhance your profile picture:

If you want to add some flair and fun to your profile picture, you can use filters, frames, and stickers to enhance it. Filters, frames, and stickers are optional features that allow you to apply different effects, borders, and decorations to your profile picture. You can access these features by clicking on the camera icon on your profile picture and choosing from the available options.

Some tips for using filters, frames, and stickers to enhance your profile picture are:

Use filters, frames, and stickers that suit your brand and message. Avoid using filters, frames, and stickers that are inappropriate, irrelevant, or offensive. For example, do not use a filter that makes your photo look too distorted, a frame that covers your face or logo, or a sticker that contradicts your brand values or tone.

Use filters, frames, and stickers that are subtle and tasteful. Avoid using filters, frames, and stickers that are too flashy, loud, or overwhelming. For example, do not use a filter that changes your photo color too drastically, a frame that is too thick or ornate, or a sticker that is too large or animated.

Use filters, frames, and stickers that are unique and creative. Avoid using filters, frames, and stickers that are too common, boring, or generic. For example, do not use a filter that everyone else is using, a frame that is too simple or plain, or a sticker that is too cliché or predictable.

Choose a header image that supports your brand and message:

Your header image is the large rectangular image that appears behind your profile picture and name on your profile. It is one of the most prominent and noticeable features of your profile, and it can be used to showcase your brand and message more visually and creatively. Therefore, choosing a header image that supports your brand and message is crucial for creating a memorable and impactful Twitter presence.

Use a relevant, eye-catching, and well-designed image or graphic:

The first step to choosing a header image that supports your brand and message is to use a relevant, eye-catching, and well-designed image or graphic. A relevant, eye-catching, and well-designed image or graphic will capture your audience's attention and interest, and convey your brand identity and value proposition clearly and compellingly.

Some tips for using a relevant, eye-catching, and well-designed image or graphic are:

Use an image or graphic that relates to your brand and message. Avoid using an image or graphic that is unrelated, random, or confusing. For example, do not use an image of a sunset or a flower, unless they have a specific meaning or connection to your brand or message.
Use an image or graphic that is original and unique. Avoid using an image or graphic that is generic, stock, or copied. For example, do not use an image that you found on Google or a graphic that you downloaded from a free website unless you have permission or license to use it.
Use an image or graphic that is high-quality and professional. Avoid using an image or graphic that is low-quality, amateurish, or unappealing. For example, do not use an image that is blurry, pixelated, or stretched, or a graphic that is poorly designed, cluttered, or inconsistent.

Change your header image as needed to reflect your brand identity and strategy:

Your header image is not a fixed element of your profile, but a dynamic and flexible one. You can change your header image as often as you want or need to keep your profile fresh and updated and align with your brand goals and objectives.

Some reasons to change your header image are:
To celebrate a special occasion or event, such as a holiday, anniversary, or milestone.
To launch a new product or service, or to announce a new feature or update.

To promote a new offer or deal, or to highlight a benefit or advantage.
To support a cause or campaign, or to show your values or beliefs.
To showcase your achievements or awards, or to share a testimonial or feedback.
To experiment with different styles or formats, or to test different messages or audiences.

Some tips for changing your header image are:
Use a header image that is relevant and timely. Avoid using a header image that is outdated, expired, or obsolete. For example, do not use a header image that is for a past event or offer, or that is for a different season or year.
Use a header image that is clear and informative. Avoid using a header image that is vague or confusing. For example, do not use a header image that does not explain what the occasion, event, product, service, offer, deal, cause, campaign, achievement, award, testimonial, or feedback is about, or how it relates to your brand or message.
Use a header image that is engaging and inviting. Avoid using a header image that is boring or unappealing. For example, do not use a header image that does not capture your audience's attention or interest, or that does not encourage them to take action, such as follow you, visit your website, or buy your product.

To change your header image, you can:
Go to your profile and click on the Edit profile button.
Click on the camera icon on your header image.
Upload a new image from your device or choose an image from your media library.
Adjust the size and position of your image.
Click on the Apply button and then on the Save button.

You can also use third-party tools and apps to create and edit your header image, such as:
Canva
Adobe Spark
PicMonkey
Fotor
BeFunky

These tools and apps can help you:
Access a variety of templates, images, graphics, and fonts.
Customize your header image according to your preferences and needs.
Enhance your header image with filters, effects, and stickers.
Save and download your header image in different formats and sizes.

Finding and Following Relevant Accounts.

Another key step to building a strategic Twitter account is finding and following relevant accounts in your niche and industry. By doing so, you can grow your network, increase your exposure, and learn from others on the platform. You can also establish yourself as an authority and a valuable source of information in your field. Therefore, finding and following relevant accounts is essential for expanding your reach and impact on Twitter.

However, finding and following relevant accounts is not as simple as it sounds. You need to have a clear idea of who you want to follow and why. You also need to use various methods and tools to find and follow them. Moreover, you need to maintain and optimize your following over time. And most importantly, you need to engage with the accounts that you follow to build relationships and trust.

Find relevant accounts using keywords, hashtags, and lists:

One of the easiest ways to find relevant accounts is to use keywords, hashtags, and lists. Keywords are words or phrases that describe your niche, industry, or interests. Hashtags are keywords preceded by a # symbol that are used to categorize tweets. Lists are collections of accounts that are created by other users or yourself.

To find relevant accounts using keywords, hashtags, and lists, you can use the search function on Twitter. You can type in your keywords or hashtags in the search box and filter the results by accounts. You can also browse the lists that are related to your keywords or hashtags. You can then check out the profiles of the accounts that appear in the results and decide whether to follow them or not.

Some tips for finding relevant accounts using keywords, hashtags, and lists are:

Use specific and relevant keywords and hashtags that match your niche and industry. For example, if you are a digital marketer, you can use keywords like **#digitalmarketing,** **#SEO, #contentmarketing**, etc.

Use a combination of keywords and hashtags to narrow down your search. For example, if you are a digital marketer who specializes in SEO, you can use keywords like **#SEO + #digitalmarketing, #SEO + #contentmarketing**, etc.

Use quotation marks to search for exact phrases. For example, if you are looking for accounts that tweet about digital marketing tips, you can use quotation marks to search for that exact phrase.

Use the advanced search function to refine your search by location, language, date, etc. For example, if you are looking for accounts that tweet about digital marketing in Nigeria, you can use the advanced search function to filter by location and language.

Follow the lists that are created by other users who are in your niche and industry. For example, if you are a digital marketer, you can follow the lists that are created by other digital marketers.

Create your lists of accounts that you find relevant and useful. For example, you can create a list of accounts that tweet about SEO, a list of accounts that tweet about content marketing, etc. You can then follow these lists and share them with others.

Use Twitter's suggestions, trends, and topics to discover new accounts:

Another way to find relevant accounts is to use Twitter's suggestions, trends, and topics. Suggestions are accounts that Twitter recommends to you based on your profile, activity, and interests. Trends are topics that are popular or trending on Twitter at a given time. Topics are categories of interest that you can follow to see tweets related to them.

To use Twitter's suggestions, trends, and topics to discover new accounts, you can use the following features on Twitter:

Who to follow: This is a feature that shows you a list of accounts that Twitter thinks you might like to follow. You can find it on the right sidebar of your home page or the following page **https://twitter.com/following**. You can also refresh the list to see more suggestions or click on **View all** to see more accounts.

Explore: This is a feature that shows you what's happening on Twitter, including trends, topics, news, events, etc. You can find it on the left sidebar of your home page or on the explore page **https://twitter.com/explore**. You can also customize your explore page by choosing your location and interests.

Topics: This is a feature that allows you to follow topics of interest, such as sports, entertainment, politics, etc. You can find it on the left sidebar of your home page or the topics page **https://twitter.com/i/topics**. You can also browse and search for topics that you want to follow or see the topics that you are already following.

Some tips for using Twitter's suggestions, trends, and topics to discover new accounts are:
Follow the accounts that Twitter suggests to you if they are relevant and interesting to you. You can also check out their profiles, tweets, and followers to learn more about them.

Follow the trends that are related to your niche and industry. You can also click on the trends to see the tweets and accounts that are tweeting about them. You can then follow the accounts that are influential, active, and engaging in your field.

Follow the topics that are relevant and interesting to you. You can also see the tweets and accounts that are tweeting about the topics that you follow. You can then follow the accounts that are influential, active, and engaging in your field.

Follow accounts that are influential, active, and engaging in your field.

One of the most important things to consider when finding and following relevant accounts is their influence, activity, and engagement. Influence refers to the authority, credibility, and popularity of an account in a certain field. Activity refers to the frequency, recency, and consistency of an account's tweets. Engagement refers to the interaction, feedback, and conversation that an account has with its followers and other users.

To follow accounts that are influential, active, and engaging in your field, you need to evaluate their profiles, tweets, and followers. You can use the following criteria to assess whether an account is worth following or not:

Profile: A good profile should have a clear and catchy name, a relevant and professional bio, a high-quality and recognizable profile picture, a link to a website or portfolio, and a verified badge (if applicable).

Tweets: A good tweet should have a clear and concise message, a relevant and catchy hashtag, a link to a source or resource, a media or emoji (if applicable), and a call to action or question (if applicable).

Followers: A good follower should have a similar or complementary niche and industry, a high-quality and recognizable profile picture, a relevant and professional bio, a link to a website or portfolio, and a verified badge (if applicable).

Some tips for following accounts that are influential, active, and engaging in your field are:
Follow the accounts that have a high number of followers, retweets, likes, and replies. These are indicators of their influence, popularity, and engagement on Twitter.
Follow the accounts that tweet regularly, recently, and consistently. These are indicators of their activity, recency, and consistency on Twitter.
Follow the accounts that reply to their followers, retweet other users, and join conversations. These are indicators of their engagement, interaction, and feedback on Twitter.
Follow the accounts that share valuable and relevant information, insights, and tips in your field. These are indicators of their authority, credibility, and usefulness on Twitter.

Use tools and apps to manage and analyze your following:

One of the challenges of finding and following relevant accounts is managing and analyzing your following. Managing your following means keeping track of the accounts that you follow, organizing them into lists, and unfollowing the ones that are not relevant or useful to you. Analyzing your following means measuring the performance, impact, and growth of the accounts that you follow, as well as your account.

To use tools and apps to manage and analyze your following, you can use various third-party tools and apps that are available online. Some of the popular and useful tools and apps that you can use are:

Twitter Analytics: This is the official tool that Twitter provides to help you measure and improve your Twitter performance. You can access it on the analytics page **https://analytics.twitter.com/**. You can use it to see your tweet activity, audience insights, profile visits, impressions, engagements, etc. You can also use it to see the performance, impact, and growth of the accounts that you follow.

TweetDeck: This is a tool that Twitter provides to help you manage and monitor multiple Twitter accounts and lists. You can access it on the tweetdeck page **https://tweetdeck.twitter.com/**. You can use it to create and organize custom columns for your home timeline, notifications, messages, mentions, trends, etc. You can also use it to schedule tweets, filter tweets, and create and manage lists.

Hootsuite: This is a tool that helps you manage and optimize your social media presence across multiple platforms, including Twitter. You can access it on the hootsuite page **https://hootsuite.com/**. You can use it to schedule tweets, monitor mentions, track keywords, analyze metrics, etc. You can also use it to manage and analyze your following and the accounts that you follow.

Unfollow accounts that are irrelevant, inactive, or spammy:
One of the drawbacks of finding and following relevant accounts is that you might end up following some accounts that are irrelevant, inactive, or spammy. Irrelevant accounts are accounts that are not related to your niche and industry, or that have changed their focus or content over time. Inactive accounts are accounts that have not tweeted for a long time, or that tweet very rarely or inconsistently. Spammy accounts are accounts that tweet excessively, repetitively, or inappropriately, or that are bots or fake accounts.

To unfollow accounts that are irrelevant, inactive, or spammy, you need to review and audit your following regularly. You can use the following criteria to decide whether to unfollow an account or not:

Relevance: A good account should be relevant to your niche and industry, or to your interests and goals. You should unfollow an account if it is not related to your field, or if it has changed its focus or content over time.

Activity: A good account should be active on Twitter, or at least tweet regularly, recently, and consistently. You should unfollow an account if it has not tweeted for a long time, or if it tweets very rarely or inconsistently.

Spam: A good account should not be spammy on Twitter, or tweet excessively, repetitively, or inappropriately. You should unfollow an account if it tweets too much, too often, or too similar, or if it tweets irrelevant, offensive, or misleading content. You should also unfollow an account if it is a bot or a fake account.

Some tips for unfollowing accounts that are irrelevant, inactive, or spammy are:

Use tools and apps to help you unfollow accounts that are irrelevant, inactive, or spammy. Some of the popular and useful tools and apps that you can use are:

Unfollowspy: This is a tool that helps you manage and analyze your Twitter followers and following. You can access it on the unfollowspy page **https://unfollowspy.com/**. You can use it to see who you follow, who follows you back, who unfollowed you, who is inactive, who is spammy, etc. You can also use it to unfollow accounts that are irrelevant, inactive, or spammy.

 ManageFlitter: This is a tool that helps you manage and optimize your Twitter account. You can access it on the manageflitter page **https://manageflitter.com/**. You can use it to see who you follow, who follows you back, who unfollowed you, who is inactive, who is spammy, etc. You can also use it to unfollow accounts that are irrelevant, inactive, or spammy.

Crowdfire: This is a tool that helps you grow and manage your social media presence across multiple platforms, including Twitter. You can access it on the crowdfire page **https://www.crowdfireapp.com/**. You can use it to see who you follow, who follows you back, who unfollowed you, who is inactive, who is spammy, etc. You can also use it to unfollow accounts that are irrelevant, inactive, or spammy.

Unfollow accounts that are irrelevant, inactive, or spammy gradually and carefully. Do not unfollow too many accounts at once, or you might risk losing some of your followers or getting suspended by Twitter. Also, do not unfollow accounts that are influential, active, and engaging in your field, or you might miss out on valuable and relevant information, insights, and tips.

Unfollow accounts that are irrelevant, inactive, or spammy politely and respectfully. Do not unfollow accounts that you have a personal or professional relationship with, or that you have interacted with before, unless you have a valid reason. Also, do not unfollow accounts that have followed you recently, or that have retweeted, liked, or replied to your tweets, unless they are clearly irrelevant, inactive, or spammy.

Engage with the accounts that you follow to build relationships and trust:
One of the benefits of finding and following relevant accounts is that you can engage with them to build relationships and trust. Engaging with the accounts that you follow means interacting, communicating, and conversing with them on Twitter. You can also learn from them, share with them, and collaborate with them on Twitter.

To engage with the accounts that you follow to build relationships and trust, you need to be proactive, responsive, and genuine. You can use the following methods and tips to engage with the accounts that you follow:

Reply: A reply is a tweet that is directed to another user by mentioning their username with the @ symbol. You can use replies to answer questions, give feedback, express opinions, join conversations, etc. You can also use replies to ask questions, request feedback, seek opinions, start conversations, etc.

Retweet: A retweet is a tweet that is shared by another user with their followers. You can use retweets to show appreciation, agreement, support, endorsement, etc. You can also use retweets to share valuable and relevant information, insights, and tips with your followers.

Like: A like is a tweet that is marked with a heart symbol by another user. You can use likes to show appreciation, agreement, support, endorsement, etc. You can also use likes to bookmark tweets that you want to save or revisit later.

Mention: A mention is a tweet that includes another user's username with the @ symbol. You can use mentions to acknowledge, appreciate, thank, congratulate, etc. You can also use mentions to introduce, recommend, invite, etc.

Direct message: A direct message is a private message that is sent to another user. You can use direct messages to communicate, converse, and collaborate with other users privately. You can also use direct messages to send personal or confidential information, requests, or offers.

Some tips for engaging with the accounts that you follow to build relationships and trust are:

Engage with the accounts that are influential, active, and engaging in your field. These are the accounts that can provide you with valuable and relevant information, insights, and tips, as well as exposure and opportunities in your field.

Engage with the accounts that are responsive, interactive, and conversational. These are the accounts that can provide you with feedback, opinions, and perspectives, as well as interaction and conversation on Twitter.

Engage with the accounts that are genuine, authentic, and respectful. These are the accounts that can provide you with trust, credibility, and reputation, as well as respect and appreciation on Twitter.

Finding and following relevant accounts is one of the key steps to building a strategic Twitter account. By finding and following relevant accounts, you can grow your network, increase your exposure, and learn from others on the platform. You can also establish yourself as an authority and a valuable source of information in your field.

However, finding and following relevant accounts is not enough. You also need to manage and analyze your following, unfollow accounts that are irrelevant, inactive, or spammy, and engage with the accounts that you follow to build relationships and trust.

Defining Your Target Audience.

Defining your target audience is anothernd thing that you need to do to build a strategic Twitter account. It is also the main factor that determines the success of your Twitter income strategy. Therefore, defining your target audience and their needs and preferences is essential for creating and delivering valuable content that converts.

Identify your ideal follower persona and their characteristics:
Your ideal follower persona is a fictional representation of your ideal customer or client. It is based on the characteristics, goals, and challenges of the people who are most likely to benefit from your products or services. By creating a detailed profile of your ideal follower persona, you can better understand who you are trying to reach and what they are looking for.

To create your ideal follower persona, you need to answer some questions such as:

What is their name, age, gender, location, and occupation?
What are their hobbies, interests, values, and beliefs?
What are their pain points, problems, and frustrations?
What are their goals, aspirations, and motivations?
How do they use Twitter and other social media platforms?
What kind of content do they consume and share on Twitter?
What are their preferred tone, style, and format of communication?

You can use online tools such as HubSpot's Make My Persona **https://www.hubspot.com/make-my-persona** to create your ideal follower persona. You can also use real data from your existing customers or clients, or conduct interviews or surveys with your target market.

For example, if you are a fitness coach who offers online courses and coaching programs, your ideal follower persona might look something like this:

Name: Jessica
Age: 28
Gender: Female
Location: New York, USA
Occupation: Marketing manager
Hobbies: Yoga, reading, traveling
Interests: Health, wellness, personal development
Values: Balance, happiness, growth
Pain points: Lack of time, stress, low energy
Goals: Lose weight, get fit, improve mental health
Twitter usage: Follows fitness influencers, likes and retweets motivational quotes, watches workout videos
Content preferences: Inspirational stories, tips and tricks, challenges and giveaways
Communication preferences: Casual, friendly, positive, concise

Use Twitter analytics and surveys to understand your audience demographics and behavior:

Once you have created your ideal follower persona, you need to validate and refine it with real data from your existing or potential followers. You can use Twitter analytics and surveys to understand your audience demographics and behavior.

Twitter analytics is a free tool that provides insights into your Twitter account performance, such as:

How many followers do you have and how they change over time. How many impressions, engagements, and clicks your tweets receive.
How your followers are distributed by country, gender, and language.
What are the top interests, topics, and hashtags of your followers
How your followers compare to the average Twitter user.

You can access Twitter analytics by clicking on the More menu on the left sidebar of your Twitter profile and selecting Analytics. You can also visit **https://analytics.twitter.com/** and log in with your Twitter account.

Twitter analytics can help you understand who your current followers are and how they interact with your content. You can use this information to adjust your content strategy and optimize your tweets for maximum reach and engagement.

For example, if you find out that most of your followers are from the UK, you might want to use British English and local references in your tweets. If you find out that most of your followers are interested in sports, you might want to incorporate sports-related content or hashtags in your tweets.

Surveys are another way to understand your audience's demographics and behavior. You can use online tools such as Googlehg Forms **https://www.google.com/forms/about/**, SurveyMonkey **https://www.surveymonkey.com/**, or Typeform **https://www.typeform.com/** to create and distribute surveys to your target market. You can ask questions such as:

How did you find out about my Twitter account?
What are your main reasons for following me?

How often do you check my tweets and what do you do with them?
What kind of content do you like or dislike from me?
What are your expectations and suggestions for my Twitter account?

Surveys can help you understand what your potential followers are looking for and how you can meet their needs and preferences. You can use this feedback to improve your content quality and relevance and increase your follower loyalty and satisfaction.

For example, if you find out that most of your potential followers are looking for practical advice and guidance from you, you might want to create more educational and informative content. If you find out that most of your potential followers are looking for more interaction and engagement from you, you might want to ask more questions and polls and respond to their comments and messages.

Use social listening and feedback to understand your audience's needs and preferences:

Social listening and feedback are two methods to understand your audience's needs and preferences. Social listening is the process of monitoring and analyzing the online conversations and sentiments of your target market. Feedback is the process of collecting and evaluating the opinions and suggestions of your existing or potential customers or clients.

You can use social listening tools such as Hootsuite **https://hootsuite.com/**, Sprout Social **https://sproutsocial.com/**, or Brandwatch **https://www.brandwatch.com/** to track and measure what people are saying about you, your competitors, your industry, or your niche on Twitter and other social media platforms. You can use feedback tools such as Trustpilot **https://www.trustpilot.com/**, Yotpo **https://www.yotpo.com/**, or Testimonial Monkey **https://www.testimonialmonkey.com/** to collect and display the reviews and ratings of your products or services from your customers or clients.

Social listening and feedback can help you understand what your audience's pain points, problems, frustrations, goals, aspirations, and motivations are. You can use this information to create and deliver valuable content that solves their problems, fulfills their desires, and exceeds their expectations.

For example, if you find out that most of your audience's pain points are related to time management and productivity, you might want to create and share content that helps them plan their day, prioritize their tasks, and achieve their goals. If you find out that most of your audience's goals are related to personal growth and development, you might want to create and share content that inspires them, challenges them, and supports them.

Segment your audience into different groups based on their interests and goals:

Segmenting your audience into different groups based on their interests and goals is a way to customize and personalize your content and communication with each group. By segmenting your audience, you can:

Increase your content relevance and resonance
Improve your content performance and conversion
Enhance your audience loyalty and retention
Reduce your content creation and distribution costs

Gain a competitive edge and differentiation

You can divide your audience into different groups based on factors like:
Demographics: age, gender, location, occupation, income, etc.
Psychographics: hobbies, interests, values, beliefs, personality, etc.
Behavior: Twitter usage, content consumption, engagement, purchase, etc.
Needs: pain points, problems, frustrations, goals, aspirations, motivations, etc.

You can use tools such as Mailchimp **https://mailchimp.com/**, ConvertKit **https://convertkit.com/**, or ActiveCampaign **https://www.activecampaign.com/** to create and manage your audience segments and send them targeted and tailored content and communication via email or other channels.

For example, if you have segmented your audience into three groups based on their needs, such as:

Group A: wants to lose weight and get fit
Group B: wants to improve mental health and well-being
Group C: wants to learn new skills and hobbies

You can create and send different content and communication to each group, such as:

Group A: a weekly newsletter with workout tips, healthy recipes, and success stories
Group B: a daily tweet with motivational quotes, mindfulness exercises, and self-care tips
Group C: a monthly webinar with expert interviews, tutorials, and resources

Tailor your content and communication to each segment of your audience:

Tailoring your content and communication to each segment of your audience is the final step to defining your target audience and optimizing your Twitter income strategy. By tailoring your content and communication, you can:

Increase your content appeal and attraction
Improve your content retention and recall
Enhance your content trust and credibility
Reduce your content noise and clutter
Gain a loyal and engaged fan base and community

You can use various techniques to tailor your content and communication to each segment of your audience, such as:

Tone: the attitude and emotion that you convey through your words, such as formal, casual, humorous, serious, etc.
Style: the way that you write or speak, such as simple, complex, concise, verbose, etc.
Format: the way that you present your content, such as text, image, video, audio, etc.
Call to action: the action that you want your audience to take after consuming your content, such as liking, retweeting, commenting, subscribing, buying, etc.

You can use tools such as Grammarly **https://www.grammarly.com/,** Hemingway **http://www.hemingwayapp.com/,** or CoSchedule Headline Analyzer **https://coschedule.com/headline-analyzer** to check and improve your content tone, style, and format. You can also use tools such as Canva **https://www.canva.com/,** Lumen5

https://lumen5.com/, or Anchor **https://anchor.fm/** to create and edit your content images, videos, and audios.

For example, if you have tailored your content and communication to each segment of your audience, such as:

Group A: a weekly newsletter with workout tips, healthy recipes, and success stories
Group B: a daily tweet with motivational quotes, mindfulness exercises, and self-care tips
Group C: a monthly webinar with expert interviews, tutorials, and resources

You can use different techniques to tailor your content and communication to each group, such as:

Group A: a formal, informative, and persuasive tone, a complex and verbose style, a text and image format, and a call to action to subscribe to your online course or coaching program
Group B: a casual, friendly, and positive tone, a simple and concise style, a text and video format, and a call to action to like, retweet, or comment on your tweet
Group C: a professional, educational, and engaging tone, a moderate and clear style, a video and audio format, and a call to action to register for your webinar or download your resources

Developing Your Unique Voice and Style.

Developing your unique voice and style is the seventh and final thing that you need to do to build a strategic Twitter account. It is also the main way that you can differentiate yourself from the competition and connect with your followers on an emotional level. Therefore, developing your unique voice and style is vital for establishing your authenticity and authority on Twitter.

Define your brand voice and tone:
Your brand voice is how your brand shows its identity and tone, through the language you choose and the style you communicate. Your brand tone is the mood and attitude of your brand, expressed through the words you choose and the way you deliver them.

Your brand voice and tone should reflect your personality and values, as well as the needs and preferences of your target audience. For example, if you are a fitness coach who helps busy professionals lose weight and get in shape, your brand voice might be energetic, motivational, and confident, while your brand tone might be friendly, supportive, and encouraging.

To define your brand voice and tone, you can use the following steps:
Identify your brand values and mission. What are the fundamental values and rules that shape your brand? What is the purpose and goal of your brand?
Identify your brand personality traits. How do you want your audience to see and feel about your brand? What are the adjectives that describe your brand?

Identify your brand voice and tone attributes. How do you want your audience to perceive and relate to your brand's voice and style? What are the nouns and verbs that describe your brand? Create a brand voice and tone chart. Write down your brand values, personality traits, voice attributes, and tone attributes in a table or a diagram. Use this chart as a reference when you create your Twitter content.

Use language, grammar, and punctuation to express your voice and tone:
The language, grammar, and punctuation you use on Twitter can have a significant impact on how your voice and tone are perceived by your audience. You should use language, grammar, and punctuation that are appropriate for your brand voice and tone, as well as for the context and purpose of your tweet.

For example, if your brand voice is casual and informal, you might use slang, abbreviations, and contractions, such as **lol, btw**, and **don't**. If your brand tone is playful and humorous, you might use puns, jokes, and wordplay, such as **Don't be a quitter, be a fitter** or **You snooze, you lose**. If your brand voice is professional and authoritative, you might use formal and precise language, such as **According to the latest research** or **We recommend that you**. If your brand tone is serious and informative, you might use facts, statistics, and quotes, such as **Did you know that 75% of people who exercise regularly report higher levels of happiness?** or **As Albert Einstein once said, 'The only source of knowledge experiences'**.

You should also pay attention to the grammar and punctuation rules that apply to Twitter, such as the 280-character limit, the use of hashtags, mentions, and links, and the use of capitalization, commas, periods, and other symbols. You should use grammar and punctuation that are consistent with your brand voice and tone, as well as with Twitter etiquette and best practices. For example, if your brand voice is friendly and conversational, you might use exclamation points, question marks, and ellipses, such as **Wow, that's amazing!** or **How are you feeling today?** or **I can't wait to see you....** If your brand tone is urgent and persuasive, you might use imperative sentences, calls to action, and emojis, such as **Don't miss this opportunity!** or **Click here to sign up now!**

Use emojis, gifs, and memes to add humor and emotion to your voice and tone:
Emojis, gifs, and memes are visual elements that can enhance your voice and tone on Twitter by adding humor and emotion to your tweets. Emojis are tiny icons that represent different feelings, things, creatures, and signs. GIFs are brief, moving images that repeat endlessly. Memes are images, videos, or texts that are humorous, ironic, or satirical, and that are often modified and shared by internet users.

You can use emojis, gifs, and memes to add humor and emotion to your voice and tone on Twitter by following these tips:
Use emojis, gifs, and memes that are relevant to your brand voice and tone, as well as to the content and context of your tweet. For example, if your brand voice is fun and quirky, you might use emojis, gifs, and memes that are cute, funny, or surprising. If your brand tone is passionate and inspirational, you might use emojis, gifs, and memes that are positive, motivational, or uplifting.
Use emojis, gifs, and memes that are appropriate for your target audience, as well as for the platform and culture of Twitter. For example, if your target audience is young and trendy, you might use emojis, gifs, and memes that are popular, trendy, or viral. If your target audience is older and more conservative, you might use emojis, gifs, and memes that are classic, simple, or respectful.

Use emojis, gifs, and memes sparingly and strategically, as too many or too frequent use of them can dilute your message, distract your audience, or annoy your followers. For example, you might use emojis, gifs, and memes to emphasize a point, express a feeling, add some humor, or create some engagement, but not to replace your words, overstate your emotions, make fun of others, or spam your followers.

Develop your brand style and how it reflects your message and goals:
Your brand style is the visual identity of your brand, expressed through the colors, fonts, and images you use on your Twitter account. Your brand style should reflect your message and goals, as well as the personality and values of your brand.

Your brand style can help you create a consistent and coherent image of your brand, as well as attract and retain the attention of your audience. You can develop your brand style by following these steps:

Choose a color palette that suits your brand voice and tone, as well as your message and goals. Context and culture influence how people perceive and associate colors with different things. For example, red can signify passion, excitement, or danger, while blue can signify trust, calm, or professionalism. You should choose colors that convey the emotions and values that you want your audience to feel and associate with your brand. You should also choose colors that are complementary, contrasting, or harmonious, to create a pleasing and balanced visual effect.
Choose a font that suits your brand voice and tone, as well as your message and goals. Fonts can have different styles and characteristics, depending on the shape, size, and weight of the letters. For example, serif fonts can signify tradition, elegance, or

authority, while sans-serif fonts can signify modernity, simplicity, or clarity. You should choose a font that matches the personality and character of your brand, as well as the mood and attitude of your brand. You should also choose a font that is legible, readable, and scalable, to ensure that your text is clear and visible on different devices and screens.

Choose images that suit your brand voice and tone, as well as your message and goals. Images can have different types and formats, depending on the content, quality, and purpose of the pictures. For example, photos can signify realism, authenticity, or emotion, while illustrations can signify creativity, imagination, or humor. You should choose images that support and enhance your message and goals, as well as the personality and values of your brand. You should also choose images that are original, relevant, and high-quality, to ensure that your pictures are attractive and professional.

Use consistency and coherence to reinforce your voice and style: Consistency and coherence are the key elements that can reinforce your voice and style on Twitter, as well as create a strong and memorable impression of your brand. Consistency means using the same or similar voice and style across all your tweets and interactions, while coherence means using the same or similar voice and style across all your platforms and channels.

You can use consistency and coherence to reinforce your voice and style on Twitter by following these tips: Use a consistent and coherent profile picture, cover photo, bio, and username, as these are the first things that your audience will see and remember about your brand. Your profile picture, cover photo, bio, and username should reflect your brand voice and tone, as well as your message and goals. They should also be consistent and coherent with your other platforms and channels, such as your website, blog, or email.

Use a consistent and coherent tone, language, and format for your tweets, as these are the main things that your audience will read and engage with. Your tone, language, and format should reflect your brand voice and tone, as well as your message and goals. They should also be consistent and coherent with your other tweets and interactions, such as your replies, retweets, or likes.

Use a consistent and coherent theme, topic, and purpose for your tweets, as these are the main things that your audience will expect and appreciate from your brand. Your theme, topic, and purpose should reflect your brand voice and tone, as well as your message and goals. They should also be consistent and coherent with your other platforms and channels, such as your website, blog, or email.

By following the steps and tips outlined in this chapter, you will be able to create and optimize your Twitter account for maximum impact and income potential. You will have a professional and appealing Twitter account that sets you apart from the crowd and positions you as an expert and influencer in your field. This will enable you to leverage the power of Twitter to generate income and grow your online business.

Chapter Two

Follower Acquisition and Retention Tactics.

Twitter is a powerful tool for personal branding, marketing, networking, and social impact, as it allows you to reach and engage with a large and diverse audience. However, to succeed on Twitter, you need to have a clear strategy for acquiring and retaining followers who are interested in your content and value proposition.

In this chapter, we will explore the various tactics and best practices that you can use to grow and sustain your follower base on Twitter. We will cover the following topics:

Creating and sharing valuable and relevant content that solves problems, educates, entertains, or inspires your followers. We will discuss how to identify your target audience, craft your unique voice and message, and produce high-quality content that aligns with your goals and brand identity.
Use multimedia formats such as images, videos, GIFs, polls, and live streams to enhance your content and increase engagement. We will explain how to leverage the different types of media that Twitter supports, and how to optimize them for maximum impact and reach.
Interacting with your followers and other users by liking, commenting, retweeting, and direct messaging. We will demonstrate how to build and maintain relationships with your followers, as well as how to expand your network and influence

by engaging with other relevant users and influencers in your niche.

Participating in Twitter chats, events, and challenges to network and showcase your expertise. We will show you how to find and join relevant conversations and communities on Twitter, and how to contribute value and gain visibility and credibility through them.

Using analytics tools to measure your performance and identify areas of improvement. We will introduce you to the various metrics and tools that you can use to track and analyze your Twitter activity and results, and how to use them to refine and improve your strategy and tactics.

Implement best practices to maintain and grow your follower base, such as posting consistently, using calls to action, and avoiding spamming. We will summarize the key dos and don'ts of Twitter etiquette and best practices, and how to avoid common pitfalls and mistakes that can harm your reputation and follower retention.

By the end of this chapter, you will have a comprehensive and practical guide on how to effectively use Twitter to attract and retain followers who are interested in your content and value proposition. You will also have the skills and tools to monitor and evaluate your progress and performance and to adjust and optimize your strategy and tactics accordingly.

Creating and Sharing Valuable and Relevant Content.

Content is the core of any digital marketing strategy. It is how you communicate your message, showcase your expertise, and build trust with your audience. But not all content is created equal. To stand out from the noise and attract your ideal customers, you need to create and share content that is valuable and relevant to them.

What is valuable and relevant content?
Valuable and relevant content is content that meets the needs, interests, and goals of your target audience. It is content that:

Solves a problem they have or answers a question they ask.
Educate them on a topic they want to learn more about.
Entertain them with a story they can relate to or enjoy.
Inspires them with a vision they aspire to or a challenge they want to overcome.

Valuable and relevant content is not content that:

Is generic, boring, or irrelevant to your niche
Is overly promotional, sales, or self-serving
Is outdated, inaccurate, or misleading
Is poorly written, formatted, or designed

Why is valuable and relevant content important?
Creating and sharing valuable and relevant content is important for several reasons:

It helps you attract and retain your ideal customers. By providing them with content that matches their needs and interests, you can capture their attention, earn their trust, and persuade them to take action.

It helps you establish your authority and credibility. By demonstrating your knowledge, skills, and experience, you can position yourself as an expert and a leader in your field.

It helps you differentiate yourself from your competitors. By offering content that is unique, original, and engaging, you can showcase your personality, voice, and value proposition.

It helps you optimize your online presence and performance. By using content that is optimized for search engines, social media, and mobile devices, you can increase your visibility, reach, and conversions.

What are some examples of valuable and relevant content?
There are many types of content that you can create and share to provide value and relevance to your audience. Some of the most popular and effective ones are:

Blog posts: Blog posts are articles that you publish on your website or a third-party platform. They are ideal for sharing your insights, opinions, tips, or case studies on a specific topic or issue.

Infographics: Infographics display data, facts, and information visually. They are ideal for simplifying complex concepts, highlighting key points, or comparing different options or scenarios.

Podcasts: Podcasts are audio recordings that you distribute online. They are ideal for sharing your stories, interviews, conversations, or advice on a specific theme or niche.

Ebooks: Ebooks are digital books that you offer for free or for a fee. They are ideal for providing in-depth knowledge, guidance, or solutions to a specific subject or problem.

Videos: Videos are moving images that you upload on your website or a video-sharing platform. They are ideal for showing your products, services, or processes, demonstrating your skills or results, or entertaining your audience with humor or emotion.

What steps can you take to make and share content that is both meaningful and appealing to your target market?

Creating and sharing valuable and relevant content requires planning, research, creativity, and execution.
These are some helpful suggestions and effective strategies for you:
Know your audience: Before you create any content, you need to understand who your target audience is, what they want, and how they consume content. You can use methods like surveys, interviews, analytics, or personas to access and understand information about your readers:

Define your goals: After you know your audience, you need to define what you want to achieve with your content. You can use the SMART approach to define specific, measurable, achievable, relevant, and time-bound objectives for your content. specific, measurable, achievable, relevant, and time-bound goals for your content.

Choose your topics: Based on your audience and your goals, you need to choose topics that are relevant, interesting, and valuable to your audience. You can use tools such as keyword research, social media listening, or content analysis to find and validate topics for your content.

Create your content: Once you have your topics, you need to create your content using the appropriate format, style, and tone for your audience and your platform. You can use tools such as content templates, writing tools, or design tools to help you create high-quality content.

Share your content: After you create your content, you need to share it with your audience using the right channels, platforms, and methods. You can use tools such as email marketing, social media marketing, or content distribution to help you share your content effectively.

How to measure and improve your content?
Creating and sharing valuable and relevant content is not a one-time activity. It requires you to constantly check, measure, and refine it. You can follow these guidelines and proven methods to assist you:

Track your metrics: To measure the effectiveness of your content, you need to track and analyze metrics that reflect your goals. You can use tools such as Google Analytics, Facebook Insights, or YouTube Analytics to collect and report data on your content performance.

Gather feedback: To understand the impact of your content, you need to gather feedback from your audience and your stakeholders. You can use tools such as surveys, comments, reviews, or testimonials to solicit and listen to feedback on your content quality, relevance, and value.

Optimize your content: Based on your metrics and feedback, you need to optimize your content to improve its results. You can use tools such as A/B testing, content auditing, or content updating to test and refine your content elements, such as headlines, keywords, images, etc.

Creating and sharing valuable and relevant content is a key skill for any digital marketer. It can help you attract and retain your ideal customers, establish your authority and credibility, differentiate yourself from your competitors, and optimize your online presence and performance. To create and share valuable and relevant content, you need to follow a systematic process that involves knowing your audience, defining your goals, choosing your topics, creating your content, sharing your content, measuring your content, and improving your content. By following these steps and using the tips and tools suggested, you can create and share content that delivers value and relevance to your audience and your business.

Using Multimedia Formats to Enhance Your Content and Increase Engagement.

Twitter is a social network that lets users post brief messages, called tweets, to their fans. Tweets can include text, images, videos, GIFs, polls, and live streams. These are called multimedia formats, and they can help you enhance your content and increase engagement on Twitter.

Why are multimedia formats important?
Multimedia formats are important for attracting and retaining followers on Twitter for several reasons:

They help you capture attention: Multimedia formats can make your tweets stand out from the text-only tweets in your followers' timelines. They can also aid you in delivering your message more effectively and imaginatively.

They help you increase engagement: Multimedia formats can encourage your followers to interact with your tweets, such as liking, retweeting, commenting, voting, or watching. They can also help you generate more impressions, clicks, and conversions.

They help you build relationships: Multimedia formats can help you showcase your personality, voice, and values. They can also help you connect with your followers on an emotional level, such as making them laugh, smile, or feel inspired.

What are the advantages and disadvantages of multimedia formats?

There are many multimedia formats that you can use on Twitter, each with its advantages and disadvantages.
Here are some of the most common ones:

Images: Images are static pictures that you can upload or attach to your tweets. They are ideal for showing your products, services, or results, highlighting key facts or statistics, or expressing your emotions or opinions.
Advantages: Images are easy to create and share, and they can attract attention and convey information quickly and clearly.
Disadvantages: Images can take up space and bandwidth, and they can be ignored or overlooked if they are not relevant, interesting, or appealing.

Videos: Videos are moving images that you can upload or attach to your tweets. They are ideal for demonstrating your skills or processes, telling your stories or testimonials, or entertaining your audience with humor or emotion.
Advantages: Videos are engaging and immersive, and they can deliver complex or detailed messages in a short time and in a memorable way.
Disadvantages: Videos can be time-consuming and costly to produce and share, and they can be skipped or abandoned if they are not captivating, informative, or valuable.

GIFs: GIFs are animated images that you can upload or attach to your tweets. They are ideal for adding humor, personality, or emotion to your tweets, or for illustrating a simple concept or action.
Advantages: GIFs are fun and catchy, and they can add variety and spice to your tweets.
Disadvantages: GIFs can be distracting or annoying, and they can lose quality or clarity if they are too long or too large.

Polls: Polls are interactive questions that you can create and attach to your tweets. They are ideal for gathering feedback, opinions, or preferences from your followers, or for sparking a conversation or a debate.

Advantages: Polls are interactive and engaging, and they can help you learn more about your audience and their needs and interests.

Disadvantages: Polls can be biased or inaccurate, and they can be misused or abused by trolls or bots.

Live streams: Live streams are real-time broadcasts that you can create and share on Twitter using Periscope. They are ideal for showing your behind-the-scenes, hosting a Q&A session, or covering a live event or breaking news.

Advantages: Live streams are authentic and spontaneous, and they can help you build trust and rapport with your audience and create a sense of urgency and excitement.

Disadvantages: Live streams can be unpredictable and risky, and they can be affected by technical issues or external factors.

How to use multimedia formats effectively?
Using multimedia formats on Twitter is not enough to ensure success. You need to use them effectively, meaning that you need to choose the right format for your message, optimize the quality and size, add captions and descriptions, and more.

Here are some examples of how to use multimedia formats effectively:

Choose the right format for your message: Depending on your goal, audience, and topic, you need to select the format that best suits your message. For example, if you want to show how your product works, you can use a video or a GIF. If you want to share a statistic or a quote, you can use an image or a text. If you want to ask for feedback or opinions, you can use a poll or a live stream.

Optimize the quality and size. To ensure that your multimedia formats load fast and look good on different devices and screens, you need to optimize the quality and size of your files. For example, you can use tools such as Photoshop, Canva, or Giphy to edit, crop, resize, or compress your images, videos, or GIFs. You can also follow the platform guidelines for the optimal dimensions and formats for each type of multimedia.

Add captions and descriptions. To make your multimedia formats more accessible and understandable, you need to add captions and descriptions to your files. For example, you can use tools such as YouTube, Rev, or Kapwing to add subtitles, transcripts, or closed captions to your videos or live streams. You can also use the alt text feature on Twitter to add descriptions to your images or GIFs.

Use hashtags, keywords, and mentions. To make your multimedia formats more discoverable and relevant, you need to use hashtags, keywords, and mentions in your tweets. For example, you can use hashtags to categorize your content, keywords to optimize your content for search engines, and mentions to tag or acknowledge other users or accounts.

How to measure and improve your multimedia formats?
Using multimedia formats on Twitter is not a one-time activity. This process requires you to continuously observe, assess, and enhance your performance. To assist you, we have compiled some useful advice and guidelines.
Here are some tips and best practices to help you:

Track your metrics: To measure the effectiveness of your multimedia formats, you need to track and analyze metrics that reflect your goals and your audience's behavior. You can use tools such as Twitter Analytics, Twitter Media Studio, or Twitter Dashboard to collect and report data on your multimedia performance, such as impressions, engagements, views, retention, etc.

Gather feedback. To understand the impact of your multimedia formats, you need to gather feedback from your audience and your peers. You can use tools such as Twitter Polls, Twitter Spaces, or Twitter DMs to solicit and listen to feedback on your multimedia quality, relevance, and value.

Optimize your multimedia formats. Based on your metrics and feedback, you need to optimize your multimedia formats to improve their results. You can use tools such as Twitter Ads, Twitter Cards, or Twitter Fleets to test and refine your multimedia elements, such as thumbnails, titles, descriptions, etc.

Using multimedia formats to enhance your content and increase engagement on Twitter is a key skill for any digital marketer. It can help capture attention, increase engagement, and build relationships with your audience. To use multimedia formats effectively, you need to follow a systematic process that involves choosing the right format for your message, optimizing the quality and size, adding captions and descriptions, using hashtags, keywords, and mentions, tracking your metrics, gathering feedback, and optimizing your multimedia formats. By following these steps and using the tips and tools suggested, you can use multimedia formats to deliver content that is valuable and relevant to your audience and your business.

Interacting with Your Followers and Other Users.

Twitter is a social media platform that allows you to share your thoughts, opinions, and experiences with the world. But it is not enough to just post your tweets and hope that they will reach your target audience. You also need to interact with your followers and other users on Twitter to build and maintain relationships with them.

Interaction is essential for creating a sense of community and belonging among your followers and other users. By interacting with them, you show that you care about their feedback, opinions, and interests. You also demonstrate that you are not just a one-way broadcaster, but a two-way communicator who is willing to listen and engage.

Interacting with your followers and other users also brings many benefits to your personal or professional brand.
Some of the benefits are:

Increasing your reach: When you interact with your followers and other users, you increase the chances of your tweets being seen by more people. This is because interaction boosts the algorithm that determines the visibility of your tweets on the platform. Interaction also encourages your followers and other users to share your tweets with their networks, expanding your reach even further.

Increasing your engagement: Interaction also increases the level of engagement with your tweets. Engagement refers to your followers and other users' actions on your tweets, such as liking, commenting, retweeting, and direct messaging. Engagement shows that your tweets are relevant, interesting, and valuable to your audience. It also helps you measure the impact and effectiveness of your tweets.

Increasing your credibility: Interaction also enhances your credibility as a person or a brand on Twitter. Credibility refers to the trust and respect that your followers and other users have for you. By interacting with them, you show that you are knowledgeable, reliable, and honest. You also show that you are human, not a bot or a spammer. Credibility helps you build a loyal and supportive fan base that will follow you for a long time.

There are many ways to interact with your followers and other users on Twitter. Some of the common ways are:
Liking: Liking is the simplest and quickest way to interact with your followers and other users. It shows that you appreciate their tweets and acknowledge their presence. You can like any tweet that you find interesting, informative, or entertaining by clicking on the heart icon below the tweet.

Commenting: Commenting is another way to interact with your followers and other users. It lets you express your thoughts, opinions, or questions on their tweets. You can comment on any tweet that you want to respond to by clicking on the speech bubble icon below the tweet and typing your message.

Retweeting: Retweeting is a way to interact with your followers and other users by sharing their tweets with your followers. It shows that you support their tweets and want to spread their message. You can retweet any tweet that you want to share by clicking on the two arrows icon below the tweet and choosing either Retweet or Retweet with comment.

Direct messaging: Direct messaging is a way to interact with your followers and other users privately. It allows you to have a one-on-one or group conversation with them. You can direct message any user that you follow or that follows you by clicking on the envelope icon on their profile page and typing your message.

While interacting with your followers and other users on Twitter, you should also follow some tips and best practices to make your interaction more effective and enjoyable.
Some of the tips and best practices are:

Be responsive: You should try to respond to your followers and other users as soon as possible when they interact with you. This shows that you value their time and attention and that you are attentive and active on the platform. You should also try to answer their questions, address their concerns, and thank them for their compliments or feedback.

Be authentic: You should be yourself when you interact with your followers and other users. You should not pretend to be someone else or say something that you do not mean. You should also avoid using automated or generic responses that sound impersonal or robotic. You should use your voice and tone that reflects your personality and brand identity.

Be respectful: You should be respectful of your followers and other users when you interact with them. You should not insult, harass, or bully them. You should also not spam them with unwanted or irrelevant messages. You should respect their opinions and preferences, even if they differ from yours. You should also respect their privacy and personal information, and not share them without their consent.

Avoid arguments and trolls: You should avoid getting into arguments and conflicts with your followers and other users when you interact with them. You should not engage with users who are rude, aggressive, or abusive. You should also not feed the trolls, who are users who deliberately provoke or annoy others for their amusement. You should ignore or block them, and report them if necessary.

Interacting with your followers and other users on Twitter is a vital part of your social media strategy. It helps you build and maintain relationships with them, and also brings many benefits for your personal or professional brand. By following the tips and best practices mentioned above, you can make your interaction more effective and enjoyable. Happy tweeting!

Participating in Twitter Chats, Events, and Challenges.

Twitter is a powerful platform for connecting with people who share your interests, passions, and goals. One of the ways to engage with your Twitter community is by participating in Twitter chats, events, and challenges. These are online conversations or activities that are organized around a specific topic, hashtag, or date. They can help you grow your follower base, showcase your expertise, and learn from others.

What are Twitter chats, events, and challenges?
Twitter chats are scheduled discussions that take place on Twitter, usually at a regular time and frequency, such as weekly or monthly. They are moderated by a host who asks questions and invites participants to share their thoughts, opinions, and experiences using a common hashtag. For example, **#ContentWritingChat** is a weekly chat that covers topics related to content writing and marketing. Twitter chats are a great way to interact with experts, influencers, and peers in your niche, and to stay updated on the latest trends, tips, and best practices.

Twitter events are live-tweeting sessions that happen during a specific event, such as a conference, webinar, product launch, or TV show. They are often hosted by the organizers or sponsors of the event, who encourage attendees or viewers to join the conversation using a designated hashtag. For example, **#INBOUND2021** is the official hashtag for the INBOUND 2021 conference, where speakers and attendees can tweet about the sessions, keynotes, and networking opportunities. Twitter events are a great way to get access to exclusive content, insights, and announcements, and to connect with like-minded people who are attending or following the event.

Twitter challenges are fun and creative activities that challenge participants to complete a task or achieve a goal using Twitter. They are usually run by influencers, brands, or communities who set the rules and rewards for the challenge. For example, **#100DaysOfCode** is a popular challenge that encourages developers to code for at least an hour every day for 100 days and tweet their progress using the hashtag. Twitter challenges are a great way to improve your skills, showcase your work, and get feedback and support from others who are taking the challenge.

What are the benefits of participating in Twitter chats, events, and challenges?

Expand your network: By joining Twitter chats, events, and challenges, you can connect with people who have similar interests, goals, or backgrounds as you. You can follow them, reply to them, retweet them, or mention them in your tweets. You can also use tools like **Twiends** to find and join relevant chats, events, and challenges in your niche. By expanding your network, you can increase your chances of finding new opportunities, collaborations, or referrals.

Showcase your expertise: By participating in Twitter chats, events, and challenges, you can demonstrate your knowledge, skills, and experience in your field. You can answer questions, share insights, provide feedback, or offer solutions. You can also use tools like **Buffer** to schedule your tweets, optimize your timing, and track your performance. By showcasing your expertise, you can establish your authority, credibility, and reputation in your niche, and attract more followers, clients, or customers.

Gain exposure: By participating in Twitter chats, events, and challenges, you can increase your visibility and reach on Twitter.

You can use hashtags, keywords, and mentions to attract attention and engagement from your target audience. You can also use tools like **99signals** to find and join the best chats, events, and challenges for marketers. By gaining exposure, you can grow your brand awareness, generate more traffic, leads, or sales, and expand your influence.

How to participate in Twitter chats, events, and challenges?
Find relevant opportunities: To participate in Twitter chats, events, and challenges, you need to find the ones that match your interests, goals, and availability. You can use tools like **TweetChat** or **Twubs** to search for hashtags, topics, or hosts. You can also follow influencers, brands, or communities that run or promote chats, events, and challenges in your niche. You can also use tools like **Google Alerts** or **TweetDeck** to monitor and discover new chats, events, and challenges related to your keywords or industry.

Prepare beforehand: To participate in Twitter chats, events, and challenges, you need to prepare yourself and your Twitter account. You can research the topic, host, or organizer of the chat, event, or challenge. You can also update your bio, profile picture, and pinned tweet to reflect your personal or professional brand. You can also create a list of tweets, links, or media that you want to share during the chat, event, or challenge. You can also use tools like **Canva** or **Pablo** to create eye-catching images or graphics for your tweets.

Contribute value: To participate in Twitter chats, events, and challenges, you need to contribute value to the conversation or activity. You can tweet your answers, opinions, or experiences using the hashtag. You can also ask questions, give compliments, or provide feedback to other participants. You can also use media, such as images, videos, or GIFs, to enhance your tweets. You can also use tools like **Bitly** or **Sniply** to shorten or customize your links, and to add calls to action or tracking codes to your tweets.

Follow up afterward: To participate in Twitter chats, events, and challenges, you need to follow up with the people and the content that you interacted with. You can thank the host, organizer, or influencer for running or promoting the chat, event, or challenge. You can also follow, reply, retweet, or mention the participants that you connected with. You can also use tools like **Twitter Analytics** or **Sprout Social** to measure your impact, engagement, and growth. You can also use tools like **Storify** or **Wakelet** to curate and share the highlights of the chat, event, or challenge.

What are the tips and best practices for participating in Twitter chats, events, and challenges?
Be active: To participate in Twitter chats, events, and challenges, you need to be active and consistent. You can join as many chats, events, and challenges as you can, as long as they are relevant and valuable to you. You can also tweet frequently, but not excessively, during the chat, event, or challenge. You can also use tools like **Hootsuite** or **Tweetbot** to manage multiple chats, events, and challenges at the same time, and to switch between different accounts or devices.

Be polite: To participate in Twitter chats, events, and challenges, you need to be polite and respectful. You can use proper grammar, spelling, and punctuation in your tweets. You can also avoid using profanity, sarcasm, or negativity. You can also express gratitude and recognition for the work of others. You can also use tools like **Grammarly** or **Hemingway** to check and improve your writing, and to avoid errors or mistakes in your tweets.

Be professional: To participate in Twitter chats, events, and challenges, you need to be professional and authentic. You can use your real name, photo, and bio in your Twitter account. You can also tweet in a way that reflects your personal or professional brand, values, and goals. You can also use tools like **Brand24** or **Mention** to monitor and manage your online reputation and to respond to any mentions or feedback about you or your brand.

Avoid self-promotion: To participate in Twitter chats, events, and challenges, you need to avoid self-promotion and spamming. You can avoid tweeting links to your products, services, or website unless they are relevant and helpful to the topic or task. You can also avoid using hashtags, keywords, or mentions that are unrelated or inappropriate to the chat, event, or challenge. You can also use tools like **SocialOomph** or **Crowdfire** to avoid sending automated or repetitive tweets and to avoid violating Twitter's rules or policies.

Using Analytics Tools to Measure Your Performance and Identify Areas of Improvement:

Analytics tools are software applications that allow you to collect, measure, and analyze data from your Twitter account. They can help you track and improve your follower acquisition and retention tactics by providing you with valuable insights into your Twitter performance.

Analytics tools can offer some advantages such as:
You can understand your audience better by knowing who they are, where they are from, what they are interested in, and how they interact with your content.
You can evaluate your content quality and effectiveness by seeing how many impressions, clicks, likes, retweets, replies, and mentions your tweets generate, and how they compare to your competitors or industry benchmarks.
You can optimize your engagement strategy by finding out the best times and frequencies to post, the optimal length and format of your tweets, the most relevant hashtags and keywords to use, and the most influential users to connect with.
You can identify your strengths and weaknesses by discovering what works and what doesn't for your Twitter goals, and what areas you need to improve or focus on.

Some examples of how to use analytics tools are:
Set SMART (Specific, Measurable, Achievable, Relevant, and Time-bound) goals for your Twitter account, such as increasing your followers by 10% in a month, or boosting your engagement rate by 5% in a week.

Choose the right metrics to track your progress and performance, such as follower growth, reach, impressions, engagement rate, click-through rate, conversion rate, etc.

Analyze the data from your analytics tools and look for patterns, trends, correlations, and anomalies. For instance, you can see which tweets performed well or poorly, which topics or keywords generated the most interest or feedback, which users or influencers mentioned or retweeted you, etc.

Make data-driven decisions and take actions based on your analysis. For example, you can tweak your content strategy, adjust your posting schedule, experiment with different formats or media, engage with your audience more, collaborate with other users or brands, etc.

Some tips and best practices for using analytics tools are:
Use reliable and relevant tools that suit your needs and goals. There are many analytics tools available, both free and paid, that offer different features and functionalities. Some of the popular ones are Twitter Analytics, Hootsuite, Buffer, Sprout Social, etc.

Review your results regularly and consistently. You should monitor your analytics tools at least once a week, or more frequently if you have active campaigns or events. You should also compare your results over time and across different platforms or channels.

Make data-driven decisions and take actions based on your analysis. For example, you can tweak your content strategy, adjust your posting schedule, experiment with different formats or media, engage with your audience more, collaborate with other users or brands, etc.

In this chapter, we have explored various follower acquisition and retention tactics on Twitter, such as:

Creating and sharing valuable and relevant content that solves problems, educates, entertains, or inspires your followers.
Use multimedia formats such as images, videos, GIFs, polls, and live streams to enhance your content and increase engagement.
Interacting with your followers and other users by liking, commenting, retweeting, and direct messaging.
Participating in Twitter chats, events, and challenges to network and showcase your expertise.
Using analytics tools to measure your performance and identify areas of improvement.
Implementing best practices to maintain and grow your follower base, such as posting consistently, using calls to action, and avoiding spamming

These tactics can help you attract, connect, and interact with your potential and existing followers, and ultimately convert them into loyal customers and advocates for your brand.

However, acquiring and retaining followers is not a one-time event, but an ongoing process that requires consistent effort and improvement. To maintain and grow your follower base on Twitter, you should follow these best practices:

Post regularly and at optimal times
Use clear and compelling calls to action in your tweets
Provide value and relevance to your followers
Be prompt and polite when responding to comments and messages
Avoid spamming, over-promoting, or being too salesy

Try out various kinds of content and formats.
Monitor and measure your performance and results.
Learn from your successes and failures and adjust accordingly.

By implementing these best practices, you can build a strong and lasting relationship with your followers, and increase your brand awareness, credibility, and authority on Twitter.

Chapter Three

Optimizing Impressions.

One of the most powerful features of Twitter is its ability to connect users with relevant and timely information, opinions, and conversations. Whether you are looking for news, entertainment, education, or inspiration, you can easily find and join the online discussions that interest you. However, with millions of tweets posted every day, how can you make sure that your voice is heard and that your content reaches your target audience?

The answer lies in using **hashtags, keywords**, and **trending topics** effectively. These are the tools that help you categorize, optimize, and amplify your tweets, as well as discover and participate in the hottest and most popular topics on Twitter. By understanding how these elements work and how to use them strategically, you can increase your impressions, engagement, and influence on the platform.

In this chapter, you will learn:

The role and function of hashtags, keywords, and trending topics on Twitter. You will gain a clear understanding of what these elements are, how they are generated and ranked, and how they affect the visibility and reach of your tweets.
How to research and select the most relevant and popular hashtags, keywords, and trending topics for your niche and content. You will discover the best practices and tools for finding and choosing the most suitable and effective hashtags, keywords, and trending topics for your goals and audience.

How to incorporate hashtags, keywords, and trending topics into your tweets and bio naturally and strategically. You will learn how to craft compelling and optimized tweets and bios that include the right amount and combination of hashtags, keywords, and trending topics, without compromising the quality and clarity of your message.

How to create and join hashtag campaigns, challenges, and movements to increase your exposure and influence. You will explore the various ways and benefits of initiating and participating in hashtag-based activities and events that can boost your impressions, engagement, and followers, as well as showcase your expertise, values, and personality.

How to monitor and analyze the performance and impact of your hashtags, keywords, and trending topics. You will find out how to measure and evaluate the results and outcomes of your hashtag, keyword, and trending topic strategies, using various metrics and tools, and how to adjust and improve them accordingly.

How to avoid common mistakes and pitfalls when using hashtags, keywords, and trending topics, such as overusing, misusing, or abusing them. You will be aware of the potential risks and drawbacks of using hashtags, keywords, and trending topics inappropriately or excessively, and how to prevent and overcome them.

By the end of this chapter, you will have the knowledge and skills to optimize your impressions on Twitter using hashtags, keywords, and trending topics, and to leverage them to grow your brand and online presence.

Understanding the role and function of hashtags, keywords, and trending topics on Twitter:

Twitter is a social media platform that allows users to share short messages, called tweets, with their followers and the public. Tweets can contain text, images, videos, links, and other media. Twitter also has features that enable users to discover and join conversations about topics that interest them, such as hashtags, keywords, and trending topics. We will define what these features are and how they work on Twitter, explain how they can help you reach your target audience, increase your visibility, and boost your engagement, and provide examples of successful and unsuccessful use of these features by different types of Twitter users.

What are hashtags, keywords, and trending topics on Twitter?
Hashtags are how tweets are organized by topic, and they are words or phrases that begin with a **#** symbol. For example, **#COVID19** is a hashtag that is used to label tweets about the coronavirus pandemic. Users can click on a hashtag to see other tweets that use the same hashtag or search for a hashtag to find tweets that match their interests. Hashtags can be created by anyone and can be used for various purposes, such as raising awareness, expressing opinions, promoting events, joining movements, or having fun.

Keywords are words or phrases that are used to describe the content of a tweet. For example, **vaccine** is a keyword that can be used to indicate that a tweet is about the COVID-19 vaccine. Users can use keywords to search for tweets that contain specific terms or to filter tweets by relevance, popularity, or location. Keywords can also be used to optimize tweets for search engines and increase their chances of being found by potential followers or customers.

Trending topics are topics that are popular or newsworthy on Twitter at a given time. They are determined by an algorithm that analyzes the number and frequency of tweets that mention a certain word, phrase, hashtag, or event. Trending topics are displayed on the sidebar of the Twitter homepage and can be customized by location and interest. You can click on a trending topic to see the tweets that are related to it or join the conversation by using the same term or hashtag in their tweets. Trending topics can reflect the current mood, opinion, or interest of the Twitter community, or highlight important issues, events, or stories that are happening around the world.

How can hashtags, keywords, and trending topics help you reach your target audience, increase your visibility, and boost your engagement on Twitter?
Using hashtags, keywords, and trending topics strategically can help you achieve various goals on Twitter, such as:

Reaching your target audience: By using hashtags and keywords that are relevant to your niche, industry, or topic, you can attract the attention of users who are interested in the same things as you. For example, if you are a travel blogger, you can use hashtags like **#TravelTuesday**, **#Wanderlust**, or **#BucketList**, or keywords like **travel tips, best destinations**, or **travel photography** to reach potential followers who are looking for travel-related content. Similarly, by using trending topics that are related to your niche, industry, or topic, you can tap into the existing conversations and expose your tweets to a larger and more diverse audience. For example, if you are a health expert, you can use trending topics like **#WorldHealthDay,** **#MentalHealthAwareness,** or

#VaccineRollout to share your insights, opinions, or advice on health-related issues that are popular or important on Twitter.

Increasing your visibility: By using hashtags and keywords that are popular, specific, or unique, you can increase the chances of your tweets being seen by more users, both on and off Twitter. For example, if you are a musician, you can use hashtags like **#NewMusicFriday**, **#NowPlaying**, or **#MusicMonday**, or keywords like **new album**, **live performance**, or **music video** to showcase your latest work, to attract new fans, or generate buzz. Similarly, by using trending topics that are timely, relevant, or controversial, you can increase the exposure of your tweets to users who are following the news, events, or stories that are happening on Twitter. For example, if you are a politician, you can use trending topics like **#ElectionResults**, **#Brexit**, or **#BlackLivesMatter** to express your views, positions, or policies on political issues that are hot or important on Twitter.

Boosting your engagement: By using hashtags and keywords that are engaging, interactive, or fun, you can increase the likelihood of your tweets getting likes, replies, retweets, or shares from other users. For example, if you are a comedian, you can use hashtags like **#JokeOfTheDay**, **#FunnyFriday**, or **#RoastMe**, or keywords like **funny story**, **prank**, or **meme** to entertain your followers, make them laugh, or challenge them to roast you. Similarly, by using trending topics that are interesting, surprising, or amusing, you can increase the interest of your tweets to users who are looking for something new, different, or entertaining on Twitter. For example, if you are a celebrity, you can use trending topics like **#Oscars**, **#SuperBowl**, or **#AprilFools** to share your reactions, opinions, or jokes on entertainment, sports, or culture events that are popular or fun on Twitter.

What are some examples of successful and unsuccessful use of hashtags, keywords, and trending topics by different types of Twitter users?

Here are some examples of how different types of Twitter users have used hashtags, keywords, and trending topics successfully or unsuccessfully on Twitter:

Successful use: A famous example of successful use of hashtags, keywords, and trending topics on Twitter is the **#IceBucketChallenge** campaign, which was launched in 2014 to raise awareness and funds for amyotrophic lateral sclerosis (ALS), a neurodegenerative disease. The campaign involved people filming themselves dumping a bucket of ice water over their heads, nominating others to do the same, and donating to the ALS Association. The campaign went viral on Twitter and other social media platforms, with millions of people, including celebrities, politicians, and athletes, participating and sharing their videos using the hashtag **#IceBucketChallenge**. The campaign also used keywords like **ALS**, **donate**, or **challenge** to describe the purpose and the action of the campaign, and became a trending topic on Twitter for several weeks. The campaign was successful in raising awareness and funds for ALS, as well as generating positive publicity and engagement for the participants and the cause.

Unsuccessful use: A notorious example of unsuccessful use of hashtags, keywords, and trending topics on Twitter is the **#AskJPM** campaign, which was launched in 2013 by JPMorgan Chase, a multinational banking and financial services company. The campaign involved inviting Twitter users to ask questions to one of the company's executives, using the hashtag **#AskJPM**. The campaign was intended to be a public relations stunt to improve the company's image and reputation, which had been damaged by various scandals and lawsuits. However, the campaign backfired on Twitter, as thousands of users used the hashtag **#AskJPM** to mock, criticize, or attack the company and its executive, using keywords like **fraud**, **bailout**, or **corruption** to describe the company's practices and actions, and making the campaign a trending topic on Twitter for the wrong reasons. The campaign was unsuccessful in improving the company's image and reputation and instead generated negative publicity and backlash for the company and its executives.

Researching and selecting the most relevant and popular hashtags, keywords, and trending topics for your niche and content.

Hashtags, keywords, and trending topics are essential elements of Twitter marketing, as they help you reach your target audience, increase your visibility, and boost your engagement. However, not all hashtags, keywords, and trending topics are equally effective for your niche and content. Therefore, you need to research and select the ones that are most relevant and popular for your specific goals and audience. We will describe the tools and methods you can use to research and identify the best hashtags, keywords, and trending topics for your niche and content, explain how to evaluate their popularity, relevance, and competition, and provide tips and best practices on how to choose the right number, combination, and variation of hashtags, keywords, and trending topics for your tweets and bio.

Tools and methods for researching hashtags, keywords, and trending topics:
There are various tools and methods you can use to research and identify the best hashtags, keywords, and trending topics for your niche and content. Some examples of the ones that are often used and beneficial are:

Twitter Search: You can use Twitter's search function to find out what hashtags, keywords, and topics are currently popular or relevant for your niche and content. You can filter your search by location, language, date, and type of content (tweets, people, photos, videos, news, etc.). Advanced search operators can also help you narrow down your search and find more relevant results. For example, you can use quotation marks to search for exact phrases or use the minus sign to exclude certain terms from your search. You can also use hashtags, keywords, or topics as search terms to see how they are used by other users and how they perform in terms of engagement and reach.

Twitter Trends: You can also use Twitter's own trends feature to discover the most popular and relevant topics and hashtags for your niche and content. You can access Twitter trends from the Explore tab on your desktop or mobile app, or the sidebar on your home page. You can customize your trends settings to show you trends based on your location, language, and interests. You can also see the number of tweets and the context for each trend, and click on them to see the related tweets and conversations. Twitter trends can help you find timely and topical hashtags, keywords, and topics that you can use to join ongoing discussions and attract more attention to your content.

Hashtag and Keyword Research Tools: There are also various third-party tools that you can use to research and identify the best hashtags and keywords for your niche and content. These tools can help you find relevant, popular, and low-competition hashtags and keywords that you can use to optimize your tweets and bio. Some of the most popular and effective hashtag and keyword research tools are:

Hashtagify: Hashtagify is a tool that helps you find, analyze, and monitor hashtags and keywords for Twitter and Instagram. You can use Hashtagify to search for any hashtag or keyword and see its popularity, trends, related hashtags, influencers, and usage patterns. You can also use Hashtagify to compare different hashtags and keywords and see their performance and correlation. Hashtagify can help you find the best hashtags and keywords for your niche and content, and track their impact and effectiveness over time.

RiteTag: RiteTag is a tool that helps you find and optimize hashtags and keywords for Twitter and Instagram. You can use RiteTag to search for any hashtag or keyword and see its color-coded rating based on its potential reach, engagement, and competition. You can also use RiteTag to generate hashtag suggestions based on your images, text, or URL, and see their live stats and examples. RiteTag can help you find the best hashtags and keywords for your niche and content, and optimize them for maximum exposure and results.

Keyword Tool: Keyword Tool is a tool that helps you find and analyze keywords for Twitter and other platforms. You can use the Keyword Tool to search for any keyword and see its popularity, trends, related keywords, and questions. You can also use Keyword Tool to filter your results by location, language, and platform, and export your data to CSV or Excel. Keyword Tool can help you find the best keywords for your niche and content, and understand the search intent and behavior of your audience.

Evaluating the popularity, relevance, and competition of hashtags, keywords, and trending topics.

Once you have a list of potential hashtags, keywords, and trending topics for your niche and content, you need to evaluate them based on their popularity, relevance, and competition. These three factors can help you determine how effective and suitable they are for your Twitter marketing goals and audience.

Here are the steps to evaluate them:

Popularity: Popularity refers to how frequently and widely a hashtag, keyword, or topic is used or searched for on Twitter and other platforms. Popularity can indicate how much interest and attention a hashtag, keyword, or topic can generate for your content, and how much exposure and reach it can provide for your account. However, popularity can also imply how much competition and noise you have to face when using a hashtag, keyword, or topic, and how difficult it is to stand out and get noticed. Therefore, you need to balance popularity with relevance and competition and avoid using hashtags, keywords, or topics that are too popular or too obscure for your niche and content. You can use the tools and methods mentioned above to measure the popularity of hashtags, keywords, and topics, and look at metrics such as **volume**, **frequency**, **trends**, and **engagement**.

Relevance: Relevance refers to how closely and appropriately a hashtag, keyword, or topic matches your niche, content, goals, and audience. Relevance can indicate how well a hashtag, keyword, or topic can convey the message and purpose of your content, and how well it can attract and resonate with your target audience. However, relevance can also imply how narrow and specific a hashtag, keyword, or topic is, and how limited its scope and appeal are. Therefore, you need to balance relevance with popularity and competition and avoid using hashtags, keywords, or topics that are too generic or too niche for your niche and content. You can use your knowledge and judgment to assess the relevance of hashtags, keywords, and topics, and look at factors such as **context**, **intent**, and **alignment**.

Competition: Competition refers to how many and how strong the other users and accounts are that are using or targeting the same hashtag, keyword, or topic as you. Competition can indicate how challenging and demanding it is to use a hashtag, keyword, or topic effectively, and how likely it is to achieve your desired results and outcomes. However, competition can also imply how valuable and rewarding a hashtag, keyword, or topic is, and how much potential and opportunity it offers. Therefore, you need to balance competition with popularity and relevance and avoid using hashtags, keywords, or topics that are too competitive or too easy for your niche and content. You can use the tools and methods mentioned above to evaluate the competition of hashtags, keywords, and topics, and look at metrics such as **rank**, **difficulty**, and **performance**.

Tips and best practices for choosing hashtags, keywords, and trending topics:
After you have evaluated the popularity, relevance, and competition of hashtags, keywords, and trending topics, you need to choose the ones that are most suitable and effective for your tweets and bio.
Here are some tips and best practices for choosing hashtags, keywords, and trending topics:

Use a mix of hashtags, keywords, and trending topics: You can use a combination of hashtags, keywords, and trending topics to optimize your tweets and bio for different purposes and audiences. For example, you can use hashtags to categorize your content and join relevant communities, keywords to describe your content and target specific queries, and trending topics to capitalize on current events and conversations. You can also use different types of hashtags, keywords, and trending topics, such as brand, industry, niche, location, event, or campaign-specific ones, to diversify your content and reach.

Use the right number of hashtags, keywords, and trending topics: You can use as many hashtags, keywords, and trending topics as you want, as long as they are relevant and appropriate for your content and audience. However, you should also consider the length and readability of your tweets and bio, and avoid using too many or too few hashtags, keywords, and trending topics that can clutter or dilute your message and impact. As a general rule of thumb, you can use up to three hashtags, keywords, and trending topics per tweet, and up to 10 hashtags, keywords, and trending topics per bio.

Use the right variation and combination of hashtags, keywords, and trending topics: You can use different variations and combinations of hashtags, keywords, and trending topics to optimize your tweets and bio for different platforms and algorithms. For example, you can use capitalization, punctuation, spelling, and abbreviations to create different variations of hashtags, keywords, and trending topics, such as **#TwitterMarketing, #twittermarketing, #Twitter_Marketing, #Twitter-marketing, #twitmarketing,** etc. You can also use different combinations of hashtags, keywords, and trending topics to create different phrases and expressions, such as **#TwitterMarketingTips, #TwitterMarketingStrategy,**

#TwitterMarketing2023, etc. You can use these variations and combinations to increase your chances of being found and seen by different users and searches.

Use the right placement and order of hashtags, keywords, and trending topics: You can use different placements and orders of hashtags, keywords, and trending topics to optimize your tweets and bio for different formats and preferences. For example, you can place your hashtags, keywords, and trending topics at the beginning, middle, or end of your tweets.

Use the right placement and order of hashtags, keywords, and trending topics: You can use different placements and orders of hashtags, keywords, and trending topics to optimize your tweets and bio for different formats and preferences. For example, you can place your hashtags, keywords, and trending topics at the beginning, middle, or end of your tweets and bio, depending on the emphasis and readability you want to create. You can also order your hashtags, keywords, and trending topics by their importance, popularity, or relevance, depending on the impact and attention you want to generate.

By following these tips and best practices, you can research and select the most relevant and popular hashtags, keywords, and trending topics for your niche and content, and use them effectively to enhance your Twitter marketing strategy and results.

Incorporating hashtags, keywords, and trending topics into your tweets and bio naturally and strategically:

Twitter is a powerful platform for sharing your ideas, opinions, and stories with a large and diverse audience. However, with millions of tweets posted every day, how can you make sure that your voice is heard and that your message reaches the right people? One of the ways to do that is to use hashtags, keywords, and trending topics in your tweets and bio naturally and strategically. We will explain what these terms mean, how they can help you attract attention, convey your message, and encourage interaction.

How to use hashtags, keywords, and trending topics in your tweets and bio?

Using hashtags, keywords, and trending topics in your tweets and bio can help you achieve several goals, such as:

Attracting attention: By using hashtags, keywords, and trending topics that are relevant to your tweet and bio, you can increase the chances of your tweet and profile being seen by more users who are interested in those topics. This can help you gain more followers, likes, retweets, and replies, and grow your online presence and influence.

Conveying your message: By using hashtags, keywords, and trending topics that are clear and descriptive, you can communicate your message more effectively and efficiently. This can help you express your opinions, emotions, and personality, and make your tweet and bio more engaging and memorable.

Encouraging interaction: By using hashtags, keywords, and trending topics that are popular and timely, you can invite more users to join the conversation and share their views and experiences. This can help you create a sense of community and connection, and foster meaningful and respectful dialogue.

However, using hashtags, keywords, and trending topics in your tweets and bio also requires some skill and strategy, as not all of them are equally effective and appropriate. Here are some examples of effective and ineffective use of hashtags, keywords, and trending topics in tweets and bio by different types of Twitter users:

Personal user: A personal user is someone who uses Twitter for personal purposes, such as sharing their thoughts, feelings, hobbies, or daily activities with their friends and family. For a personal user, effective use of hashtags, keywords, and trending topics in their tweets and bio would be:
Tweet: Just finished reading #TheMidnightLibrary by @matthaig1 and I loved it! Such a beautiful and inspiring story about life, choices, and regrets. #bookreview
Bio: Avid reader, coffee lover, and traveler. Always looking for new books to read and places to visit. #bookworm #wanderlust

In this example, the user uses hashtags and keywords that are relevant to their tweet and bio, and that describe the main topic and theme of their book review. The user also tags the author of the book, which can help them get noticed and appreciated by the author and other fans. The user also uses hashtags that reflect their personality and interests, and that can help them connect with other users who share those passions.

Ineffective use of hashtags, keywords, and trending topics in their tweets and bio would be:

Tweet: OMG this book is amazing!!! #bestbookever #mustread #bookstagram #booklover #booknerd #bookaddict #bookaholic #bookworm #bookish #bibliophile #reading #reader #read #books #book #fiction #fantasy #adventure #romance #thriller #mystery #horror #comedy #drama #action #sci-fi #historical #biography #autobiography #memoir #nonfiction #selfhelp #inspirational #motivational #educational #spiritual #religious #philosophical #political #social #cultural #environmental #artistic #literary #classic #modern #contemporary #awardwinning #bestselling #newrelease #TheMidnightLibrary @matthaig1
Bio: I love books.

In this example, the user uses too many hashtags and keywords that are vague, generic, and irrelevant to their tweet and bio. The user also does not provide any specific or meaningful information about the book or their opinion of it. The user also uses a very short and bland bio that does not convey their personality or interests. The user's tweet and bio are likely to be ignored or overlooked by other users, as they are too long, cluttered, and boring.

Professional user: A professional user is someone who uses Twitter for professional purposes, such as promoting their business, brand, or product, or providing information, advice, or service to their customers or clients. For a professional user, effective use of hashtags, keywords, and trending topics in their tweets and bio would be:
Tweet: Are you looking for a new and exciting way to learn English? Check out our latest podcast episode, where we talk about the benefits of learning English through music. #LearnEnglish #EnglishPodcast #EnglishMusic.

Bio: We are a team of experienced and qualified English teachers who offer online courses, podcasts, and resources to help you improve your English skills. #EnglishTeachers #OnlineEnglish

In this example, the user uses hashtags and keywords that are relevant to their tweet and bio, and that describe the main topic and purpose of their podcast episode. The user also uses hashtags that are popular and searchable among their target audience, and that can help them attract more potential customers or clients. The user also uses a bio that summarizes their business, brand, or product, and that highlights their credentials and value proposition.

Ineffective use of hashtags, keywords, and trending topics in their tweets and bio would be:

Tweet: Listen to our new podcast episode now! #podcast #episode #new #listen #now
Bio: We teach English.

In this example, the user uses hashtags and keywords that are irrelevant to their tweet and bio, and that do not describe the main topic and purpose of their podcast episode. The user also uses hashtags that are too common and generic, and that can not help them stand out from the crowd or reach their target audience. The user also uses a bio that is too vague and brief, and that does not communicate their business, brand, or product, or their credentials and value proposition.

Influencer user: An influencer user is someone who uses Twitter to influence or inspire other users, such as celebrities, public figures, or experts in a certain field or niche. For an influencer user, effective use of hashtags, keywords, and trending topics in their tweets and bio would be:

Tweet: Today is #WorldMentalHealthDay, and I want to share with you some of the ways that I cope with stress and anxiety. Here are my top 5 tips: 1) Meditate for 10 minutes every morning. 2) Exercise for at least 30 minutes every day. 3) Write down 3 things that I am grateful for every night. 4) Talk to a friend or a therapist when I feel overwhelmed. 5) Listen to soothing music or watch a funny show when I need a break. What are your tips? #MentalHealth #SelfCare
Bio: I am a singer, songwriter, and activist. I use my voice and platform to raise awareness and support for various causes, such as mental health, human rights, and environmental issues. #Singer #Songwriter #Activist

In this example, the user uses hashtags and keywords that are relevant to their tweet and bio, and that describe the main topic and message of their tweet. The user also uses a trending topic that is timely and important, and that can help them reach a wider audience and show their expertise and credibility. The user also provides useful and practical tips that can help their followers improve their mental health and well-being and invites them to share their tips, which can increase engagement and interaction. The user also uses a bio that introduces their identity and role, and that showcases their achievements and values.

Ineffective use of hashtags, keywords, and trending topics in their tweets and bio would be:

Tweet: #WorldMentalHealthDay #MentalHealth #SelfCare #Stress #Anxiety #Depression #Happiness #Wellness #Health #Tips #Advice #Meditation #Exercise #Gratitude #Therapy #Music #Comedy #Break #Cope #Share #Follow #Like #Retweet #Reply
Bio: Follow me.

In this example, the user uses only hashtags no keywords or trending topics in their tweet, and no hashtags or keywords in their bio. The user also does not provide any content or message in their tweet and only uses hashtags that are too broad and generic, and that do not convey any specific or meaningful information. The user also uses a bio that is too short and vague, and that does not introduce their identity or role, or showcase their achievements or values. The user's tweet and bio are likely to be dismissed or ignored by other users, as they are too spammy, empty, and unprofessional.

Tips and best practices on how to balance the use of hashtags, keywords, and trending topics with the quality and clarity of your content:
As you can see from the examples above, using hashtags, keywords, and trending topics in your tweets and bio can have different effects depending on how you use them. Therefore, it is important to balance the use of hashtags, keywords, and trending topics with the quality and clarity of your content, and to follow some of the tips and best practices below:

Be relevant: Use hashtags, keywords, and trending topics that are relevant to your tweet and bio, and that match the topic, theme, or event that you are talking about. Avoid using hashtags, keywords, and trending topics that are unrelated, misleading, or inappropriate, as they can confuse or annoy your audience, and damage your reputation and credibility.

Be specific: Use hashtags, keywords, and trending topics that are specific and descriptive, and that capture the main idea or message of your tweet and bio. Avoid using hashtags, keywords, and trending topics that are too vague or general, as they can dilute or obscure your content, and make it harder for your audience to find and follow you.

Be selective: Use hashtags, keywords, and trending topics that are popular and timely, and that can help you reach a wider and more relevant audience. However, do not use too many hashtags, keywords, and trending topics, as they can clutter or overwhelm your content, and make it less readable and engaging. A good rule of thumb is to use no more than two or three hashtags, keywords, and trending topics per tweet and no more than five or six per bio.

Be original: Use hashtags, keywords, and trending topics that are unique and creative, and that reflect your personality and voice. However, do not use hashtags, keywords, and trending topics that are too obscure or complex, as they can alienate or confuse your audience, and make it difficult for them to understand and relate to you. A good way to create original hashtags, keywords, and trending topics is to combine or modify existing ones, or to use catchy phrases or slogans that summarize your content.

By following these tips and best practices, you can use hashtags, keywords, and trending topics in your tweets and bio naturally and strategically, and enhance the quality and clarity of your content. This can help you achieve your goals of attracting attention, conveying your message, encouraging interaction, and making your Twitter experience more enjoyable and rewarding.

Creating and joining hashtag campaigns, challenges, and movements to increase your exposure and influence.

Twitter is a platform where you can share your thoughts, opinions, and insights with millions of people around the world. But how do you make sure that your voice is heard and that you reach the right audience for your niche, values, and goals? One of the ways to do that is by creating and joining hashtag campaigns, challenges, and movements.

What are hashtag campaigns, challenges, and movements?
Hashtag campaigns, challenges, and movements are collective actions that use a specific word or phrase preceded by a hash sign (#) to create awareness, engagement, or change around a certain topic, issue, or cause. They can be initiated by individuals, organizations, brands, celebrities, or influencers, and they can have various purposes, such as:

Raising funds or donations for a charity or a social cause.
Promoting a product, service, event, or initiative.
Celebrating a milestone, achievement, or occasion.
Educating, informing, or entertaining the public.
Expressing solidarity, support, or protest.
Inspiring, motivating, or challenging others to do something.

How can they help you grow your following, reputation, and impact on Twitter?
Creating and joining hashtag campaigns, challenges, and movements can help you grow your following, reputation, and impact on Twitter in several ways, such as:

Increasing your visibility and reach by tapping into the existing or potential interest of other users who are following or searching for the hashtag.

Establish your authority and credibility by demonstrating your knowledge, expertise, or experience on the topic, issue, or cause.

Building your network and community by connecting with other users who share your niche, values, or goals, and who may become your followers, supporters, or collaborators.

Enhancing your brand and personality by showcasing your creativity, originality, or humor through your content.

Making a difference and adding value by contributing to a meaningful or beneficial cause, or by providing useful or entertaining content to your audience.

Examples of successful and unsuccessful hashtag campaigns, challenges, and movements by different types of Twitter users:
There are many examples of successful and unsuccessful hashtag campaigns, challenges, and movements by different types of Twitter users.
Here are some of them:

Successful examples:
#IceBucketChallenge: A viral challenge that involved dumping a bucket of ice water over one's head and nominating others to do the same or donate to the ALS Association, a nonprofit organization that supports research and care for people with amyotrophic lateral sclerosis (ALS), also known as Lou Gehrig's disease. The challenge raised over $200 million for the cause and increased public awareness and support for ALS patients and families.

#BlackLivesMatter: A global movement that advocates for racial justice and equality for Black people, especially in the face of police brutality and systemic racism. The movement started as a hashtag in 2013 after the acquittal of George Zimmerman, who fatally shot Trayvon Martin, an unarmed Black teenager, in Florida. The hashtag became a rallying cry for millions of people who protested against racial violence and discrimination, and who demanded accountability and reform from the authorities and institutions.

#ShareYourRejections: A campaign that encouraged writers, artists, and other creative professionals to share their stories of rejection and how they overcame them. The campaign aimed to inspire and motivate others who faced similar challenges and to normalize the reality and inevitability of rejection in the creative industry. The campaign also generated a lot of engagement and support among the participants and the audience, who shared their tips, advice, and encouragement.

Unsuccessful examples:

#SusanAlbumParty: A promotional campaign for the release of Susan Boyle's album Standing Ovation: The Greatest Songs from the Stage in 2012. The campaign used the hashtag #susanalbumparty, which unfortunately could be read as **Su's anal bum party**, a phrase that had nothing to do with the album or the singer. The campaign backfired and became a source of mockery and ridicule, rather than hype and excitement, for the album.

#McDStories: A marketing campaign by McDonald's in 2012 that invited customers to share their positive experiences and stories at the fast-food chain using the hashtag #McDStories. The campaign was intended to showcase the quality and service of McDonald's, but instead, it attracted a lot of negative and sarcastic responses from users who shared their horror stories and complaints about the food, the staff, the hygiene, and the ethics of McDonald's. The campaign was quickly abandoned and deemed a failure by the company.

#AskELJames: A Q&A session with E.L. James, the author of the bestselling Fifty Shades of Grey series, in 2015. The session used the hashtag #AskELJames, which was supposed to generate interest and curiosity among the fans and readers of the books. However, the session was hijacked by critics and trolls who used the hashtag to ask James harsh and hostile questions about her writing style, her portrayal of BDSM, her depiction of women and consent, and her plagiarism allegations. The session turned into a PR disaster and a public humiliation for James.

Tips and best practices on how to create and join hashtag campaigns, challenges, and movements that align with your niche, values, and goals:
If you want to create and join hashtag campaigns, challenges, and movements that align with your niche, values, and goals, here are some tips and best practices that you can follow:

Do your research: Before you create or join a hashtag campaign, challenge, or movement, make sure that you understand its purpose, origin, context, and audience. Check if the hashtag is already in use, and if so, what kind of content and sentiment it is associated with. Avoid using hashtags that are irrelevant, misleading, offensive, or controversial, unless you are intentionally trying to challenge or critique them.

Be authentic: When you create or join a hashtag campaign, challenge, or movement, make sure that you are genuine and sincere in your content and message. Don't use hashtags just for the sake of gaining attention, followers, or likes, or for exploiting a trending topic or a sensitive issue. Use hashtags that reflect your niche, values, and goals, and that resonate with your audience and community. Don't be afraid to express your opinions, emotions, or experiences, but also be respectful, responsible, and ethical in your communication.

Be creative: When you create or join a hashtag campaign, challenge, or movement, make sure that you are original and innovative in your content and format. Don't just copy or repeat what others have done or said, but try to add your twist, perspective, or value. Use different types of media, such as images, videos, gifs, memes, polls, or threads, to make your content more engaging, interactive, and memorable. Use humor, irony, or sarcasm, if appropriate, to make your content more fun, witty, or provocative.

Be strategic: When you create or join a hashtag campaign, challenge, or movement, make sure that you are smart and effective in your timing, frequency, and targeting. Don't use hashtags too early or too late, but try to catch the peak of the trend or the relevance of the topic. Don't use hashtags too often or too rarely, but try to balance the quantity and quality of your content. Don't use hashtags randomly or broadly, but try to reach the right audience and influencers who can amplify your impact and influence.

Monitoring and analyzing the performance and impact of your hashtags, keywords, and trending topics:

Hashtags, keywords, and trending topics are essential elements of any successful social media strategy, especially on X (formerly Twitter), where they help you reach a wider audience, increase engagement, and stay relevant. However, to make the most of these elements, you need to monitor and analyze their performance and impact on your brand, your audience, and your goals. We will explain why this is important, how you can do it, and what you can learn from it.

Monitoring and analyzing hashtags, keywords, and trending topics can help you:
Understand your audience: By tracking what hashtags, keywords, and topics your audience is using, talking about, and interested in, you can gain valuable insights into their preferences, needs, pain points, and sentiments. This can help you create more relevant, engaging, and personalized content for them, as well as identify potential influencers, advocates, and leads.

Evaluate your performance: By measuring how your hashtags, keywords, and topics perform on X, you can assess how effective your content is in reaching, engaging, and converting your audience. You can also assess your performance by comparing it with your competitors and industry criteria, and determine your positive and negative aspects.

Optimize your strategy: By analyzing the data and insights from your hashtag, keyword, and topic tracking, you can discover what works and what doesn't, and what you can improve or change.

You can also find new opportunities, trends, and ideas to enhance your content strategy and achieve better results.

How to monitor and analyze hashtags, keywords, and trending topics?

There are various tools and methods you can use to monitor and analyze hashtags, keywords, and trending topics on X, depending on your needs and budget.

Some examples of the ones that are often seen are:

X Analytics: This is the native analytics tool that X provides for free to all users. You can access it from the X website or app, and view various metrics and data for your hashtags, keywords, and topics, such as impressions, engagements, reach, popularity, and sentiment. You can also see how your hashtags, keywords, and topics compare to others on X, and what are the most relevant ones for your brand and industry.

Sprout Social: This is a social media management software that offers comprehensive hashtag analytics and tracking services, among other features. With Sprout Social, you can view hashtag analytics for all your networks in one central location, saving you time and effort. You can also track which hashtags your audience is using, how they're performing, and what are the related topics. Additionally, you can use Sprout Listening to find out how frequently people are talking about your topic, what related terms they're using, and what the sentiment around the topic is.

Brand24: This is a brand monitoring tool that helps you measure the buzz around your brand, product, business, or keyword. It also offers hashtag tracking and analytics services, using the power of hashtags and identifying influential profiles. You can monitor hashtags across various platforms like X and Instagram, and easily track trending hashtags with volume charts. You can also receive instant notifications for changes in hashtag performance, including viral trends.

Tips and best practices for using hashtag, keyword, and topic analysis:
Here are some tips and best practices for using the data and insights from your hashtag, keyword, and topic analysis to improve your strategy and results:

Use relevant hashtags, keywords, and topics: Make sure that the hashtags, keywords, and topics you use are relevant to your brand, your industry, your audience, and your goals. Avoid using too many or too generic hashtags, keywords, and topics, as they can dilute your message and reduce your visibility. Instead, use specific, niche, and branded hashtags, keywords, and topics that can help you stand out and attract your target audience.

Experiment and test: Don't be afraid to try new hashtags, keywords, and topics, and see how they perform. You can use tools like **Flick** or **Iconosquare** to find and generate related hashtags and keywords and optimize your content strategy. You can also use A/B testing to compare different hashtags, keywords, and topics, and see which ones generate more engagement, conversions, and traffic.

Analyze and adjust: Don't just track and measure your hashtags, keywords, and topics, but also analyze and interpret the data and insights you get from them. Look for patterns, trends, anomalies, and opportunities, and use them to inform your decisions and actions. Adjust your strategy and tactics based on the feedback and results you get, and keep improving and learning.

By monitoring and analyzing the performance and impact of your hashtags, keywords, and trending topics on X, you can take your social media strategy to the next level, and achieve your goals more effectively and efficiently.

Avoiding common mistakes and pitfalls when using hashtags, keywords, and trending topics, such as overusing, misusing, or abusing them.

Hashtags, keywords, and trending topics are powerful tools that can help you reach a wider audience, join relevant conversations, and increase your brand awareness on Twitter. However, if used incorrectly, they can also backfire and damage your reputation, credibility, and engagement. We will explain the common mistakes and pitfalls that Twitter users make when using hashtags, keywords, and trending topics, such as overusing, misusing, or abusing them. We will also provide examples of the negative consequences and backlash that can result from these mistakes and pitfalls. Finally, we will provide tips and best practices on how to avoid these mistakes and pitfalls and use hashtags, keywords, and trending topics responsibly and ethically.

Overusing hashtags, keywords, and trending topics: One of the most common mistakes that Twitter users make is overusing hashtags, keywords, and trending topics in their posts. This means adding too many hashtags, keywords, or trending topics that are irrelevant, redundant, or spammy to their posts. For example, some users may add hashtags or keywords that have nothing to do with their content, just to get more exposure or clicks. Some users may also repeat the same hashtags or keywords multiple times in the same post, or use generic or vague hashtags or keywords that do not convey any specific meaning or value. Some users may also jump on trending topics that are not related to their niche, industry, or brand, just to get more attention or followers.

The problem with overusing hashtags, keywords, and trending topics is that it can make your posts look cluttered, unprofessional, and desperate. It can also annoy or confuse your audience, who may not be able to find the relevant information or message in your posts. It can also lower your reach and engagement, as Twitter's algorithm may penalize your posts for being spammy or low-quality. Moreover, it can hurt your reputation and credibility, as your audience may lose trust or interest in your brand, or perceive you as dishonest or opportunistic.

For example, in 2014, the clothing brand Gap tried to capitalize on the trending topic of Hurricane Sandy by tweeting

All impacted by #Sandy, stay safe! Shopping at Gap.com is what we'll do today. How about you?.

This tweet faced a lot of criticism and mockery for being unkind, unaware, and using a catastrophe that harmed millions of people for its benefit. Gap later deleted the tweet and apologized, but the damage was already done.

Misusing hashtags, keywords, and trending topics: Another common mistake that Twitter users make is misusing hashtags, keywords, and trending topics in their posts. This means using hashtags, keywords, or trending topics that are inappropriate, inaccurate, or misleading for their posts. For example, some users may use hashtags or keywords that are offensive, vulgar, or controversial, without considering the potential backlash or consequences. Some users may also use hashtags or keywords that are incorrect, outdated, or misspelled, without checking their validity or relevance. Some users may also use trending topics that are sensitive, complex, or controversial, without doing proper research or providing context or sources.

The problem with misusing hashtags, keywords, and trending topics is that it can make your posts look ignorant, careless, or disrespectful. It can also offend or anger your audience, who may feel insulted, deceived, or manipulated by your posts. It can also expose you to legal or ethical issues, as you may violate the terms of service, the community guidelines, or the intellectual property rights of Twitter or other parties. Furthermore, it can damage your reputation and credibility, as your audience may question your competence, integrity, or authenticity.

For example, in 2011, the fashion brand Kenneth Cole tried to use the trending topic of the Egyptian revolution by tweeting.

Millions are in uproar in #Cairo. Rumor is they heard our new spring collection is now available online at [link].

This tweet was widely condemned and ridiculed for being insensitive, inappropriate, and disrespectful of a serious political and humanitarian crisis. Kenneth Cole later deleted the tweet and apologized, but the damage was already done.

Abusing hashtags, keywords, and trending topics: Another common mistake that Twitter users make is abusing hashtags, keywords, and trending topics in their posts. This means using hashtags, keywords, or trending topics that are malicious, harmful, or unethical for their posts. For example, some users may use hashtags or keywords that are hateful, abusive, or discriminatory, to harass, bully, or intimidate other users or groups. Some users may also use hashtags or keywords that are false, deceptive, or fraudulent, to spread misinformation, propaganda, or scams. Some users may also use trending topics that are tragic, violent, or traumatic, to exploit, mock, or trivialize the suffering or loss of other people or communities.

The problem with abusing hashtags, keywords, and trending topics is that it can make your posts look cruel, malicious, or unethical. It can also harm or hurt your audience, who may feel attacked, threatened, or deceived by your posts. It can also trigger legal or ethical actions, as you may face lawsuits, fines, bans, or boycotts from Twitter or other parties. Moreover, it can ruin your reputation and credibility, as your audience may despise, reject, or report your brand, or associate you with harmful values or behaviors.

For example, in 2017, the pizza chain Papa John's tried to use the trending topic of the NFL protests by tweeting

The NFL has hurt us. We expected the NFL and its leadership to resolve this, but they did not, and we are unhappy about it. Leadership starts at the top, and this is an example of poor leadership.

This tweet was widely criticized and boycotted for being racist, divisive, and disrespectful of the players who were protesting against police brutality and racial injustice. Papa John's later deleted the tweet and apologized, but the damage was already done.

Tips and best practices on how to avoid these mistakes and pitfalls and use hashtags, keywords, and trending topics responsibly and ethically:

To avoid these common mistakes and pitfalls and use hashtags, keywords, and trending topics responsibly and ethically, here are some tips and best practices that you can follow:

Use hashtags, keywords, and trending topics that are relevant, specific, and meaningful for your posts. Make sure that they match your content, message, and audience, and that they add value or context to your posts. Avoid using hashtags, keywords, or trending topics that are irrelevant, redundant, or spammy for your posts.

Use hashtags, keywords, and trending topics that are appropriate, accurate, and clear for your posts. Make sure that they are respectful, polite, and professional, and that they do not offend or mislead your audience. Avoid using hashtags, keywords, or trending topics that are inappropriate, inaccurate, or misleading for your posts.

Use hashtags, keywords, and trending topics that are ethical, honest, and respectful for your posts. Make sure that they are truthful, factual, and credible, and that they do not harm or exploit your audience or other parties. Avoid using hashtags, keywords, or trending topics that are unethical, dishonest, or disrespectful for your posts.

Use hashtags, keywords, and trending topics sparingly and strategically in your posts. Make sure that they are not overused or abused, and that they do not clutter or distract from your posts. Avoid using more than two hashtags per post, as this is considered the best practice by Twitter[4]. Also, avoid using hashtags or keywords in your username, bio, or profile picture, as this is considered spammy by Twitter.

Use hashtags, keywords, and trending topics carefully and wisely in your posts. Make sure that you do your research, check your sources, and cite your references, before using hashtags, keywords, or trending topics in your posts. Avoid using hashtags, keywords, or trending topics that you are not familiar with, or that you do not understand or agree with. Also, avoid using hashtags, keywords, or trending topics that are sensitive, complex, or controversial, unless you have a valid reason and a respectful tone.

By following these tips and best practices, you can use hashtags, keywords, and trending topics effectively and efficiently on Twitter. You can also avoid the common mistakes and pitfalls that can backfire and damage your brand. You can also enhance your reach, engagement, and awareness on Twitter, and build a positive and trustworthy relationship with your audience.

In this chapter, we have explored how to optimize impressions on Twitter by using hashtags, keywords, and trending topics effectively. We have learned that these elements are essential for increasing the visibility, reach, and engagement of your tweets and profile, as well as for connecting with your target audience and influencers in your niche. We have also discussed how to research and select the most relevant and popular hashtags, keywords, and trending topics for your content, and how to incorporate them into your tweets and bio naturally and strategically. Moreover, we have examined how to create and join hashtag campaigns, challenges, and movements to boost your exposure and influence, and how to monitor and analyze the performance and impact of your hashtags, keywords, and trending topics. Finally, we have identified some common mistakes and pitfalls to avoid when using hashtags, keywords, and trending topics, such as overusing, misusing, or abusing them.

By following the guidelines and best practices presented in this chapter, you will be able to optimize your impressions on Twitter and grow your brand, business, or cause. However, optimizing impressions is not the only goal of a successful Twitter strategy.

Chapter Four

Optimizing Conversions.

Twitter is one of the most popular and influential social media platforms in the world, also a powerful tool for generating income, whether you are a business, a brand, an influencer, or an individual. But how do you turn your Twitter followers into paying customers, subscribers, or supporters? How do you measure the effectiveness of your Twitter marketing efforts? The answer is **conversions.**

Conversions are the actions that you want your Twitter audience to take after seeing your content. They can be anything from clicking a link, signing up for a newsletter, downloading an app, buying a product, donating to a cause, or joining a community. Conversions are important for Twitter income because they indicate that your audience is interested, engaged, and loyal to your offer. They also help you track your return on investment (ROI) and optimize your Twitter strategy.

In this chapter, we will show you how to optimize conversions on Twitter using proven strategies and best practices. We will cover the following topics:

Creating compelling calls to action (CTAs): A CTA is a word or phrase that tells your followers what you want them to do next, such as "buy now", "sign up", "learn more", etc. A good CTA can motivate your followers to click on your links, visit your website, or take any other action you desire. We will teach you how to craft effective CTAs that capture attention, generate curiosity, and create urgency.

Offering value and incentives: To persuade your followers to take action, you need to offer them something valuable in exchange. This could be a product, a service, a freebie, a discount, a bonus, a contest, or anything else that appeals to their needs, wants, or interests. We will show you how to create and promote irresistible offers that your followers can't refuse.

Building trust and credibility: Trust is the foundation of any successful relationship, especially in the online world. If your followers don't trust you, they won't buy from you, subscribe to you, or follow your recommendations. Therefore, you need to establish yourself as a credible and trustworthy source of information, solutions, or entertainment. We will share with you some tips and techniques to build trust and credibility with your followers, such as providing social proof, testimonials, reviews, guarantees, etc.

Measuring and improving your conversion rate: To optimize conversions, you need to track and analyze your results. You need to know how many of your followers are taking the desired action, and what factors are influencing their behavior. This will help you identify what is working and what is not, and make data-driven decisions to improve your performance. We will introduce you to some tools and metrics that you can use to measure and improve your conversion rate on Twitter.

According to a study by Twitter and Bain & Company, brands that achieve higher conversion rates on Twitter also enjoy higher revenue growth, customer retention, and advocacy. Some examples of successful Twitter conversions are

Netflix: The streaming giant uses Twitter to promote its original shows and movies and to drive traffic to its website and app. In 2020, Netflix gained 37 million new subscribers worldwide, partly thanks to its viral Twitter campaigns.

Nike: The sportswear brand uses Twitter to inspire and connect with its customers, and to showcase its products and values. In 2020, Nike increased its digital sales by 82%, partly thanks to its innovative Twitter campaigns.

Barack Obama: The former US president uses Twitter to share his views and opinions, and to mobilize his supporters. In 2020, Obama raised over $7.6 million for the Biden-Harris campaign through a single tweet.

By the end of this chapter, you will have a clear understanding of how to optimize conversions on Twitter and increase your Twitter income. You will be able to apply the strategies and best practices we will teach you to your own Twitter account and see the results for yourself. So, let's get started!

Creating Compelling Calls to Action.

A call to action (CTA) is a phrase or a button that prompts your audience to take a specific action, such as clicking a link, signing up for a newsletter, buying a product, or sharing your content. A CTA can motivate your audience to engage with your brand, generate leads, increase conversions, and boost your income.

However, not all CTAs are created equal. Some CTAs are more effective than others, depending on how they are written and designed. We will discuss the elements of an effective CTA, share some tips and best practices for writing and designing CTAs for Twitter, provide examples of good and bad CTAs, and analyze what makes them work or fail.

Elements of an Effective CTA.

An effective CTA should have the following elements:

Clarity: Your CTA should be clear and concise, using simple and direct language that tells your audience exactly what you want them to do and what they will get in return. Avoid vague or ambiguous words, such as **learn more**, **get started**, or **join us**. Instead, use specific and actionable verbs, such as **download**, **register, buy,** or **share**.

Urgency: Your CTA should create a sense of urgency, using words or phrases that imply a limited-time offer, a scarcity of supply, or a fear of missing out. For example, you can use words like **now, today, limited, last chance,** or **before it's gone**. You can also use numbers or deadlines to emphasize the urgency, such as **only 10 spots left, offer ends in 24 hours,** or **save 50% today only.**

Relevance: Your CTA should be relevant to your audience, your content, and your goal. Your CTA should match the tone, style, and topic of your content, and appeal to the interests, needs, and pain points of your audience. Your CTA should also align with your goal, whether it is to generate awareness, engagement, leads, sales, or loyalty. For example, if your content is about fitness tips, your CTA should not be about buying a car, but rather about downloading a fitness app, joining a fitness community, or signing up for a fitness challenge.

Value proposition: Your CTA should communicate the value proposition of your offer, and the benefit or outcome that your audience will get by taking action. Your value proposition should be specific, measurable, and desirable, and highlight how your offer is different from or better than your competitors. For example, instead of saying **buy our product**, you can say **buy our product and get a gift**, **buy our product and save 20% off your next purchase**, or **buy our product and enjoy a lifetime warranty**.

 Tips and Best Practices for Writing and Designing CTAs for Twitter:

Twitter is a social media platform that allows you to share short messages, images, videos, and links with your followers and the public. Twitter has over 300 million active users, making it a great place to promote your brand, content, and offers. However, Twitter also has some limitations and challenges, such as a 280-character limit, a fast-paced and crowded feed, and a low attention span of users. Therefore, you need to write and design your CTAs for Twitter carefully, following these tips and best practices:

Use hashtags: Hashtags are words or phrases that start with a # symbol and are used to categorize and organize tweets by topic, theme, or event. Hashtags can help you increase the visibility, reach, and engagement of your tweets, as they allow users to find and join conversations that interest them. You can use hashtags to create or join trending topics, participate in Twitter chats, run contests or campaigns, or support a cause or a movement. You can also create your own branded hashtags, to promote your brand identity, values, or slogan. For example, Nike uses the hashtag **#JustDoIt** to inspire and motivate its followers, while Coca-Cola uses the hashtag **#ShareACoke** to encourage its followers to share their products and stories. When using hashtags, make sure they are relevant, catchy, and easy to remember, and avoid using too many or irrelevant hashtags, as they can make your tweet look spammy or confusing.

Use emojis: Emojis are small icons or symbols that represent emotions, objects, animals, or activities. Emojis can help you add some personality, emotion, and humor to your tweets, as they can convey your tone, mood, or attitude. Emojis can also help you save space, as they can replace words or phrases, or emphasize your message. For example, you can use emojis to show your excitement, gratitude, or disappointment, to ask a question, to make a suggestion, or to create a list. When using emojis, make sure they are appropriate, clear, and consistent, and avoid using too many or obscure emojis, as they can make your tweet look unprofessional or confusing.

Use images: Images are visual elements that can enhance your tweets, as they can attract attention, illustrate your message, or evoke emotions. Images can also help you showcase your products, services, or offers, or provide proof, testimonials, or social proof. For example, you can use images to show your product features, benefits, or results, to share customer reviews or feedback, or to display statistics or data. When using images, make sure they are high-quality, relevant, and optimized, and avoid using images that are blurry, pixelated, or distorted, or that violate any copyright or trademark laws.

Use videos: Videos are moving images that can also enhance your tweets, as they can capture attention, demonstrate your message, or entertain your audience. Videos can also help you tell a story, explain a concept, or teach a skill. For example, you can use videos to show your product in action, to share customer stories or testimonials, or to provide tips or tutorials. When using videos, make sure they are high-quality, relevant, and optimized, and avoid using videos that are too long, boring, or irrelevant, or that have poor sound or lighting quality.

Use polls: Polls are interactive elements that allow you to ask your audience a question and provide them with two or more options to choose from. Polls can help you increase engagement, feedback, and loyalty, as they allow you to involve your audience in your content, collect their opinions or preferences, or reward them with incentives or prizes. For example, you can use polls to ask your audience about their favorite products, features, or topics, to get their feedback on your content or offers, or to run contests or giveaways. When using polls, make sure they are relevant, interesting, and easy to answer, and avoid using polls that are too frequent, complex, or sensitive, or that have biased or leading options.

Examples of Good and Bad CTAs and Analysis.

Here are some examples of good and bad CTAs for Twitter, and an analysis of what makes them work or fail:

Good CTA:

Want to learn how to grow your Twitter followers by 10x in 30 days? Download our free ebook now and get started!

This CTA is clear, urgent, relevant, and valuable, as it tells the audience exactly what they will get (a free ebook), why they should get it (to grow their Twitter followers by 10x in 30 days), and how they can get it (by downloading it now). Use an emoji to create excitement and a downward arrow to direct attention to the link.

Bad CTA:

Check out our new product. It's awesome. Click here.

This CTA needs to be more specific, exciting, relevant, and valuable, as it does not tell the audience anything about the product, why they should care about it, or what benefit they will get from it. It also uses generic and dull words, such as "check out", "new", and "awesome", and a bland link, that does not create any interest or curiosity.

Good CTA:

Last chance to join our exclusive webinar on how to master Twitter marketing in 2024! Don't miss this opportunity to learn from the experts and boost your income! Register now before it's too late!

This CTA is clear, urgent, relevant, and valuable, as it tells the audience what they will learn (how to master Twitter marketing in 2021), why they should learn it (to boost their income), and how they can learn it (by joining the webinar). It also uses emojis to create urgency and alertness, and words like **last chance**, **exclusive, don't miss**, and **before it's too late** to create a sense of scarcity and fear of missing out.

Bad CTA:

We have a webinar tomorrow. Sign up if you want.

This CTA is vague, boring, irrelevant, and valueless, as it does not tell the audience anything about the webinar, why they should sign up for it, or what benefit they will get from it. It also uses a passive and indifferent tone, such as **we have**, **if you want**, and a period, that does not create any motivation or enthusiasm.

Good CTA:

Want to win a free trip to Hawaii? All you have to do is follow us, retweet this tweet, and tag three friends in the comments! Hurry, the contest ends in 48 hours!

This CTA is clear, urgent, relevant, and valuable, as it tells the audience what they can win (a free trip to Hawaii), how they can win it (by following, retweeting, and tagging), and when they can win it (in 48 hours). It also uses emojis to create excitement and appeal, and arrows to draw attention to the CTA.

Bad CTA:

Follow us for more updates.

This CTA is vague, boring, irrelevant, and valueless, as it does not tell the audience what kind of updates they will get, why they should follow you, or what benefit they will get from following you. It also uses a generic and dull word, such as "updates", that do not create any interest or curiosity.

Creating compelling calls to action for Twitter is an important skill that can help you increase your income from this platform. By following the elements, tips, and best practices discussed in this subchapter, and by analyzing the examples of good and bad CTAs, you can write and design CTAs that motivate your audience to take action and engage with your brand, content, and offers.

Remember, a good CTA is clear, urgent, relevant, and valuable, and uses hashtags, emojis, images, videos, or polls to enhance your message and appeal to your audience.

Offering Value and Incentives.

One of the most effective ways to optimize your conversions and loyalty on Twitter is to offer value and incentives to your followers and potential customers. Value and incentives are anything that can make your audience feel appreciated, rewarded, or motivated to take action. They can also help you stand out from the competition, build trust and credibility, and increase your brand awareness and engagement.

Types of Value and Incentives:

There are many types of value and incentives that you can offer on Twitter, depending on your goals, budget, and audience. Some of the most common ones are

Free content: This can include ebooks, reports, guides, checklists, webinars, podcasts, videos, infographics, etc. that provide useful information, tips, insights, or solutions to your audience's problems or interests. Free content can help you showcase your expertise, generate leads, and educate your audience.

Discounts: This can include a percentage off, dollar off, buy one get one free, free shipping, etc. that reduce the price of your products or services. Discounts can help you boost your sales, clear your inventory, and attract new customers.

Coupons: This can include codes, vouchers, or links that can be redeemed for a discount or a free item. Coupons can help you increase your conversions, drive traffic to your website or store, and encourage repeat purchases.

Giveaways: This can include contests, sweepstakes, or raffles that offer a chance to win a prize, such as a product, a gift card, a trip, etc. Giveaways can help you grow your followers, increase your engagement, and generate buzz around your brand.

Contests: This can include competitions that require participants to submit an entry, such as a photo, a video, a caption, a review, etc. Contests can help you create user-generated content, foster community, and showcase your brand personality.

Tips and Best Practices.

To create and deliver value and incentives effectively on Twitter, here are some tips and best practices that you should follow:

Segment your audience: Not all your followers or customers have the same needs, preferences, or behaviors. You should segment your audience based on criteria such as demographics, interests, purchase history, engagement level, etc., and tailor your value and incentives accordingly. This can help you increase your relevance, personalization, and conversion rate.

Personalize your offers: You should use the data and insights that you have about your audience to create offers that match their specific needs, wants, or goals. You should also use their names, locations, or other details to make your offers more human and appealing. This can help you build rapport, trust, and loyalty with your audience.

Time your campaigns: You should consider the best time to launch your campaigns, based on factors such as seasonality, holidays, events, trends, etc. You should also test different times of the day or days of the week to see when your audience is most active and responsive. This can help you maximize your reach, exposure, and impact.

Promote your campaigns: You should use various channels and methods to promote your campaigns, such as hashtags, mentions, retweets, direct messages, email, blog, website, etc. You should also leverage your existing customers, partners, influencers, or advocates to spread the word about your campaigns. This can help you increase your visibility, awareness, and participation.

Track and measure your results: You should use tools and metrics to track and measure the performance of your campaigns, such as impressions, clicks, conversions, sales, revenue, etc. You should also collect feedback from your audience, such as comments, ratings, reviews, testimonials, etc. This can help you evaluate your effectiveness, identify your strengths and weaknesses, and optimize your future campaigns.

Examples and Analysis.

To inspire you, here are some examples of successful value and incentive campaigns on Twitter and what makes them appealing:

Netflix: Netflix is a streaming service that offers a variety of movies, shows, documentaries, etc. for a monthly fee. Netflix often offers free content on Twitter, such as trailers, clips, behind-the-scenes, interviews, etc. that showcase their original and exclusive content. Netflix also offers discounts and coupons, such as free trials, referrals, gift cards, etc. that entice new or existing customers to subscribe or renew their service. Netflix also offers giveaways and contests, such as trivia, polls, quizzes, etc. that engage their fans and reward them with prizes, such as merchandise, tickets, access, etc. Netflix's value and incentive campaigns are appealing because they provide entertainment, information, and savings to their audience, while also highlighting their unique and diverse content.

Starbucks: Starbucks is a coffee company that offers a variety of beverages, food, and merchandise. Starbucks often offers discounts and coupons on Twitter, such as happy hour, seasonal specials, loyalty rewards, etc. that offer their products or services at a lower cost. Starbucks also offers giveaways and contests, such as **#RedCupContest**, **#ShareEvent**, **#FrappuccinoFun**, etc. that invite their customers to share their experiences and creativity with their products and reward them with prizes, such as free drinks, gift cards, trips, etc. Starbucks's value and incentive campaigns are appealing because they provide convenience, variety, and fun to their customers, while also showcasing their brand culture and values.

Nike: Nike is a sports brand that offers a variety of footwear, apparel, and equipment. Nike often offers free content on Twitter, such as tips, advice, inspiration, stories, etc. that provide value and motivation to their audience. Nike also offers discounts and coupons, such as flash sales, clearance, membership, etc. that lower the price of their products or services. Nike also offers giveaways and contests, such as **#Breaking2**, **#JustDoIt**, **#NikeReact**, etc. that challenge their fans and reward them with prizes, such as products, access, recognition, etc. Nike's value and incentive campaigns are appealing because they provide support, innovation, and empowerment to their audience, while also highlighting their brand mission and vision.

Offering value and incentives is a powerful strategy to optimize your conversions and loyalty on Twitter. By providing free content, discounts, coupons, giveaways, and contests, you can attract, engage, and retain your audience, while also showcasing your brand identity and value proposition. However, to create and deliver value and incentives effectively, you need to segment your audience, personalize your offers, time your campaigns, promote your campaigns, and track and measure your results. By following these tips and best practices, you can create value and incentive campaigns that resonate with your audience and achieve your goals. You can also learn from the examples of successful value and incentive campaigns from Netflix, Starbucks, and Nike, and apply their lessons to your campaigns.

Building Trust and Credibility.

Trust and credibility are essential for any online business or personal brand. They can enhance your reputation and authority on Twitter, which can lead to more conversions, engagement, and loyalty. We will explain how building trust and credibility can benefit your Twitter presence, discuss the factors that influence them, and share some tips and best practices for achieving them. We will also provide some examples of trustworthy and credible Twitter accounts and analyze what makes them stand out.

How Building Trust and Credibility Can Benefit Your Twitter Presence.

Twitter is a powerful platform for connecting, communicating, and influencing your audience. However, to make the most of it, you need to establish trust and credibility with your followers and potential customers. Here are some of the benefits of building trust and credibility on Twitter:

It can increase your reach and visibility. Trustworthy and credible accounts tend to have more followers, retweets, likes, and mentions, which can boost your exposure and awareness on Twitter.

It can improve your reputation and authority. Trustworthy and credible accounts are seen as experts, leaders, and influencers in their niche or industry. They can build a loyal fan base, attract media attention, and gain recognition and respect from their peers and competitors.

It can enhance your customer satisfaction and loyalty. Trustworthy and credible accounts can deliver value, quality, and consistency to their customers. They can also handle customer feedback, complaints, and queries effectively and professionally.

This would enhance your ability to satisfy your customers, retain them, and earn more referrals.

It can boost your conversions and sales. Trustworthy and credible accounts can persuade and motivate their customers to take action, such as clicking a link, signing up for a newsletter, or buying a product or service. They can also leverage social proof, testimonials, reviews, ratings, endorsements, and other forms of trust signals to increase their conversion rates and sales.

Factors That Influence Trust and Credibility on Twitter.

Many factors can affect your trust and credibility on Twitter. One of them is

Your profile: Your profile is how you present yourself in the online business world. It should be compelling, clear, and consistent. It should include a high-quality profile picture, a relevant and catchy bio, a link to your website or landing page, and a pinned tweet that showcases your value proposition or a call to action.

Your content: Your content is your main communication tool. It should be valuable, relevant, and engaging. It must also have originality, accuracy, and up-to-date. You should avoid posting spammy, misleading, or offensive content that can damage your reputation and credibility.

Your engagement: Your engagement is your social interaction. It should be frequent, timely, and meaningful. You should respond to comments and mentions, join relevant conversations, use polls and questions, and acknowledge your followers and customers. You should also avoid being rude, defensive, or aggressive in your interactions.

Your consistency: Your consistency is your reliability. It should be evident in your posting frequency, timing, tone, and style. You should maintain a regular and optimal posting schedule, experiment with different posting times, and use a consistent and appropriate voice and language for your audience and niche.

Tips and Best Practices for Building and Maintaining Trust and Credibility on Twitter.

Here are some tips and best practices for building and maintaining trust and credibility on Twitter:

Be authentic and transparent: Be yourself and show your personality and values. Be honest and open about your goals, intentions, and opinions. Admit your mistakes and apologize when necessary. Don't hide or delete negative feedback, but address it constructively and respectfully.

Be helpful and informative: Provide useful and relevant information and resources to your audience. Answer their questions, solve their problems, and share your insights and expertise. Don't just promote your products or services, but educate and inform your audience.

Be respectful and courteous: Respect your audience and their views, preferences, and needs. Be polite and friendly in your communication. Don't spam, troll, or harass your audience or others on Twitter. Don't engage in arguments or controversies that can harm your reputation and credibility.

Be credible and trustworthy: Back up your claims and statements with facts, data, and sources. Don't forget to mention your references and give recognition to the ones who deserve it. Don't plagiarize, fabricate, or exaggerate your content. Don't make false or unrealistic promises or guarantees.

Be social and collaborative: Connect and network with other trustworthy and credible accounts in your niche or industry. Follow, retweet, like, and mention them. Collaborate and partner with them on projects, campaigns, or events. Don't isolate yourself or ignore your peers and competitors.

Examples of Trustworthy and Credible Twitter Accounts and What Makes Them Stand Out

There are many examples of trustworthy and credible Twitter accounts that you can learn from and emulate. Here are a few of them and what makes them unique:

@BillGates: Bill Gates is the co-founder of Microsoft and the co-chair of the Bill & Melinda Gates Foundation. He is one of the most influential and respected figures in the world. His Twitter account reflects his passion and expertise in technology, philanthropy, and global issues. He posts valuable and informative content, such as articles, videos, podcasts, and books. He also engages with his followers and other influential accounts, such as Barack Obama, Elon Musk, and Oprah Winfrey. He has over 55 million followers and a verified blue check mark.

@NASA: NASA is the National Aeronautics and Space Administration of the United States. It is the leading agency for space exploration, research, and education. Its Twitter account showcases its achievements, discoveries, and innovations in space. It posts stunning and captivating images, videos, and live streams of its missions, launches, and events. It also interacts with its followers and other relevant accounts, such as astronauts, scientists, and media outlets. It has over 46 million followers and a verified blue check mark.

@Oprah: Oprah Winfrey is a media mogul, philanthropist, and cultural icon. She is the founder and CEO of OWN, the Oprah Winfrey Network, and the host of the Oprah's Book Club and Super Soul Sunday podcasts. Her Twitter account reflects her personality and values. She posts inspirational and motivational content, such as quotes, stories, and lessons. She also engages with her followers and other celebrities, such as Michelle Obama, Ellen DeGeneres, and Reese Witherspoon. She has over 43 million followers and a verified blue check mark.

Building trust and credibility on Twitter can have many benefits for your online business or personal brand. It can increase your reach and visibility, improve your reputation and authority, enhance your customer satisfaction and loyalty, and boost your conversions and sales. To build trust and credibility on Twitter, you need to consider the factors that influence them, such as your profile, your content, your engagement, and your consistency. You also need to follow some tips and best practices, such as being authentic, helpful, respectful, credible, and social. You can also look at some examples of trustworthy and credible Twitter accounts and what makes them stand out. By applying these strategies and techniques, you can optimize your conversions and achieve your Twitter goals.

Measuring and Improving Your Conversion Rate.

If you want to optimize your Twitter income, you need to measure and improve your conversion rate. Your conversion rate is the percentage of your Twitter audience that takes a desired action, such as clicking on your link, signing up for your newsletter, buying your product, or downloading your ebook. The higher your conversion rate, the more revenue you can generate from your Twitter traffic.

But how do you measure and improve your conversion rate? We will discuss the following topics:

The metrics and tools you can use to track and analyze your conversion rate.
The tips and best practices for improving your conversion rate.
The examples of Twitter conversion rate optimization strategies and what makes them effective.

Metrics and Tools for Tracking and Analyzing Your Conversion Rate.

To measure and improve your conversion rate, you need to track and analyze the following metrics:

Impressions: The number of times your tweet is shown to your audience. This indicates how much exposure your tweet has and how many potential customers you can reach.

Clicks: The number of times your audience clicks on your link or call to action. This indicates how much interest your tweet generates and how many leads you can drive to your landing page or website.

Conversions: The number of times your audience completes the desired action, such as signing up, buying, or downloading. This indicates how much value your tweet delivers and how many customers you can acquire.

Cost per conversion: The amount of money you spend to get one conversion. This indicates how efficient your tweet is and how profitable your campaign is.

Conversion rate: The ratio of conversions to clicks, expressed as a percentage. This indicates how effective your tweet is and how well it persuades your audience to take action.

To track and analyze these metrics, you need to use some tools, such as

Twitter Analytics: This is the native tool that Twitter provides to help you monitor and measure your tweet performance. You can access it from your Twitter profile or dashboard. It shows you the impressions, clicks, engagements, and engagement rate of your tweets. You can also view the information on the demographics, interests, and actions of your audience.

Google Analytics: This is a web analytics tool that helps you measure and understand your website traffic. You can use it to track the conversions, bounce rate, time on page, and other metrics of your landing page or website. You can also set up goals and funnels to measure the steps and outcomes of your conversion process.

Bitly: This is a link-shortening and tracking tool that helps you create and manage your links. You can use it to shorten your links, customize them, and track the clicks, referrals, and locations of your link traffic. You can also integrate it with Twitter and Google Analytics to get more insights into your link performance.

By using these tools, you can get a comprehensive view of your conversion funnel, from the tweet to the landing page or website. You can also identify the strengths and weaknesses of your conversion strategy, and find out where you can improve.

Tips and Best Practices for Improving Your Conversion Rate.

To improve your conversion rate, you need to optimize your tweet, your link, and your landing page or website.
Here are some tips and best practices for each element:

Optimize your tweet: Your tweet is the first thing that your audience sees and decides whether to click or not. To make your tweet more appealing and persuasive, you should:

Use clear and concise language that communicates the benefits and value of your offer.
Include a compelling call to action that tells your audience what to do next.
Add relevant hashtags, keywords, and mentions to increase your tweet visibility and reach.
Use eye-catching images, videos, or GIFs to attract attention and convey emotion.
Test different headlines, copy, and media to see what works best for your audience.

Optimize your link: Your link is the bridge that connects your tweet and your landing page or website. To make your link more trustworthy and clickable, you should:

Use a short and descriptive link that matches your tweet and your landing page or website.

Use a custom domain or branded link that reflects your identity and authority.

Use a tracking tool like Bitly to measure and optimize your link performance.

Avoid using spammy or misleading links that may harm your reputation and conversion rate.

Optimize your landing page or website: Your landing page or website is the final destination where your audience completes the desired action. To make your landing page or website more engaging and convincing, you should:

Use a clear and consistent headline, subheadline, and copy that matches your tweet and your link.

Use a simple and intuitive design that focuses on your offer and your call to action.

Show social evidence, testimonials, or reviews to create a trustworthy and credible impression.

Use urgency, scarcity, or incentives to create a sense of FOMO (fear of missing out) and motivate action.

Test different elements, such as colors, fonts, images, buttons, etc., to see what improves your conversion rate.

By optimizing these elements, you can increase the chances of your audience clicking on your link, landing on your page or website, and taking the desired action. You can also reduce the friction and hesitation that may prevent your audience from converting.

Example of Twitter Conversion Rate Optimization Strategies and What Makes Them Effective.

To illustrate how you can measure and improve your conversion rate, let's look at some examples of Twitter conversion rate optimization strategies and analyze what makes them effective.

Example 1: A blogger who wants to grow their email list and promote their ebook. They use the following tweet:

Want to learn how to start a successful blog in 2024? Download my free ebook and get access to my exclusive newsletter with tips, tricks, and resources for #blogging. Click here: bit.ly/blog-ebook-2024.

This tweet is effective because:

 It uses clear and concise language that communicates the benefits and value of the offer.
It includes a compelling call to action that tells the audience what to do next.
It uses a relevant hashtag (#blogging) to increase the tweet visibility and reach
Use an eye-catching image of the ebook cover to attract attention and convey emotion.
It uses a short and descriptive link that matches the tweet and the landing page.
It uses a custom domain (bit.ly) that reflects the identity and authority of the blogger.
It uses a tracking tool (Bitly) to measure and optimize the link performance.
It leads to a landing page that has a clear and consistent headline, subheadline, and copy that matches the tweet and the link.
It uses a simple and intuitive design that focuses on the offer and the call to action.
It uses social proof (number of subscribers) to build trust and credibility.

It uses urgency (limited time offer) to create a sense of FOMO and motivate action.

By following these examples, you can learn how to craft effective tweets, links, and landing pages or websites that can boost your conversion rate and your Twitter income.

In this chapter, you have learned how to optimize your conversions and increase your Twitter income. We have covered the following topics:

Creating compelling calls to action: A call to action is a phrase or a button that tells your audience what to do next, such as clicking on your link, subscribing to your newsletter, purchasing your product, or downloading your ebook. A compelling call to action should be clear, concise, and persuasive, and should communicate the benefits and value of your offer.

Offering value and incentives: Value and incentives are the reasons why your audience should take action on your offer. Value is the benefit or solution that your offer provides to your audience, such as solving a problem, satisfying a need, or fulfilling a desire. Incentives are the rewards or bonuses that your offer gives to your audience, such as discounts, freebies, or guarantees. Offering value and incentives can help you attract and motivate your audience to take action.

Building trust and credibility: Trust and credibility are the factors that influence how your audience perceives you and your offer. Trust is the confidence and belief that your audience has in you and your offer, and that you will deliver what you promise. Credibility is the reputation and authority that you have in your niche or industry, and that you are an expert or a leader in your field. Building trust and credibility can help you establish and maintain a loyal and engaged audience that will take action on your offer.

Measuring and improving your conversion rate: Your conversion rate is the percentage of your Twitter audience that takes the desired action on your offer. The higher your conversion rate, the more revenue you can generate from your Twitter traffic. To measure and improve your conversion rate, you need to track and analyze the metrics and tools that show you how your tweet, your link, and your landing page or website perform. You also need to optimize these elements to make them more appealing, trustworthy, and effective.

By applying these topics, you can create and execute a successful Twitter conversion strategy that can boost your Twitter income. You can also test and experiment with different elements, such as headlines, copy, media, links, design, etc., to see what works best for your audience and your offer. Remember, conversion optimization is an ongoing process that requires constant monitoring, measuring, and improving.

Chapter Five

Proven Income Strategies.

Twitter is not only a powerful platform for sharing your thoughts, opinions, and insights with the world, but also a lucrative source of income for many users. Whether you have a large following or a niche audience, there are multiple ways to monetize your Twitter presence and turn your tweets into cash.

In this chapter, you will learn about the various income opportunities and models available on Twitter, and how to choose the ones that suit your goals, skills, and values. You will also discover how to find and partner with brands, businesses, and platforms that offer paid opportunities for Twitter users, such as sponsored tweets, product reviews, influencer campaigns, and more.

You will also learn how to create and post sponsored tweets that promote products, services, or causes authentically and ethically, without compromising your credibility and trust with your followers. You will also learn how to avoid common pitfalls and mistakes that can damage your reputation and income potential.

Moreover, you will learn how to sell your products and services through Twitter, by creating landing pages, sales funnels, and payment systems that convert your followers into customers. You will also learn how to leverage the power of social proof, testimonials, and referrals to boost your sales and revenue.

Furthermore, you will learn how to become an affiliate marketer and earn commissions by promoting other people's products and services through your tweets and bio. You will also learn how to find and join the best affiliate programs and networks, and how to create compelling and persuasive tweets that drive traffic and conversions.

Additionally, you will learn how to launch creator subscriptions and offer exclusive content and perks to your paid subscribers. You will also learn how to set up and manage your subscription service, and how to deliver value and satisfaction to your loyal fans and supporters.

Finally, you will learn how to join the X Ads Revenue Sharing Program and earn a share of the ad revenue generated by your tweets. You will also learn how to optimize your tweets for maximum reach and engagement, and how to track and measure your performance and earnings.

By the end of this chapter, you will have a clear understanding of the proven income strategies that you can use to monetize your Twitter presence and generate a steady and sustainable income from your tweets.

Sponsored Tweets.

Sponsored tweets are tweets that Twitter users pay to have promoted in the Twitter feeds of other users. By paying to promote their tweets, advertisers hope to reach a larger audience and generate more engagement (likes, retweets, etc.). Sponsored tweets are a form of influencer marketing, where influential people on social media endorse or recommend products or services to their followers.

To create and post sponsored tweets, you need to have a Twitter account and a PayPal account. You also need to register with a platform that connects advertisers with Twitter influencers, such as SponsoredTweets. Once you sign up, you can browse and apply for paid opportunities that match your interests, niche, and audience. You can also set your price and terms for each sponsored tweet. When you get accepted by an advertiser, you can create and post the sponsored tweet according to their guidelines and requirements. You will get paid through PayPal after the sponsored tweet is approved and verified by the platform.

There are different types of sponsored tweets, depending on the goal and the content of the advertiser.
Some common types are:

Product reviews: These are tweets that showcase a product or service and provide an honest opinion or feedback about it. For example, a beauty blogger might tweet a photo of herself using a makeup product and share her thoughts on its quality and performance.

Testimonials: These are tweets that endorse a brand or a business and share a positive experience or outcome. For example, a fitness influencer might tweet a video of himself doing a workout routine and thank the gym that sponsored him for helping him achieve his goals.

Giveaways: These are tweets that offer a chance to win a prize or a reward for following certain instructions or criteria. For example, a travel blogger might tweet a link to a contest page and ask her followers to enter by liking, retweeting, and commenting on her tweet.

Contests: These are tweets that challenge the followers to do something creative or fun and reward the best entries with a prize or recognition. For example, a music artist might tweet a snippet of his new song and ask his followers to make a cover or a remix of it and share it with a hashtag.

To find and partner with brands, businesses, and platforms that offer paid opportunities for Twitter users, there are some best practices and tips to follow:

Know your niche and audience: You should have a clear idea of what topics, interests, and values you and your followers share, and look for sponsors that align with them. This will help you create relevant and engaging sponsored tweets that resonate with your audience and avoid alienating them with irrelevant or inappropriate content.

Build your credibility and reputation: You should have a consistent and authentic voice and style, and post high-quality and original content that showcases your expertise and personality. This will help you attract and retain loyal followers, and impress potential sponsors with your influence and professionalism.

Research and pitch to potential sponsors: You should do some research on the brands, businesses, and platforms that offer sponsored tweets in your niche, and find out their goals, expectations, and requirements. You should also prepare a pitch that highlights your value proposition, your audience demographics and metrics, and your rates and terms. You should then reach out to them via email, direct message, or their preferred channel, and follow up until you get a response.

Negotiate and sign a contract: You should negotiate the details of the sponsorship deal, such as the number, frequency, and duration of the sponsored tweets, the content and format of the tweets, the payment method and amount, and the disclosure and disclaimer policies. You should also sign a contract that outlines the rights and responsibilities of both parties and protects you from any legal or ethical issues.

There are some tools and resources that can help you create and manage sponsored tweets, such as:

Canva: A graphic design tool that enables you to create eye-catching and professional images and videos for your sponsored tweets and other social media posts.

Grammarly: A writing assistant tool that helps you check and improve the grammar, spelling, and clarity of your sponsored tweets and other social media posts.

SponsoredTweets: This is a Twitter influencer discovery tool that helps you search for and connect with advertisers that match your niche and audience. You can also create and track your sponsored tweets, and get paid through the platform.

Hootsuite: This is a social media management tool that helps you schedule and publish your sponsored tweets, and monitor and analyze their performance and impact. You can also manage multiple Twitter accounts, and collaborate with your sponsors and team members.

Twitter Ads: This is Twitter's advertising platform that helps you create and run your own promoted tweets, and reach a wider and more targeted audience. You can also set your budget and goals, and measure and optimize your results.

Finally, there are some dos and don'ts for posting sponsored tweets that are authentic, ethical, and compliant with Twitter's policies and guidelines, such as:

Do disclose your relationship with the sponsor: You should always make it clear that your tweet is sponsored, and use hashtags like #ad, #sponsored, or #partner to indicate that. This will help you maintain your credibility and trust with your followers, and avoid misleading or deceiving them.

Don't spam your followers with too many sponsored tweets: You should balance your sponsored tweets with your regular tweets, and avoid overwhelming or annoying your followers with too much promotional content. This will help you keep your followers engaged and interested, and avoid losing them or damaging your reputation.

Do follow the rules and regulations of your niche and location: You should be aware of and comply with the laws and standards that apply to your niche and location, and respect the rights and preferences of your followers. This will help you avoid any legal or ethical issues, and protect yourself and your sponsor from any liability or backlash.

Don't compromise your integrity or values for money: You should only accept and promote sponsors that you genuinely like and trust, and that offer products or services that you have tried and tested. You should also be honest and transparent about your opinions and experiences, and avoid making false or exaggerated claims. This will help you preserve your integrity and values, and build a loyal and satisfied audience.

Selling Your Products and Services.

Twitter is not only a platform for sharing your thoughts, opinions, and insights, but also a powerful tool for generating income from your products and services. Whether you have an existing business or want to start one, you can use Twitter to create and sell your offerings, such as ebooks, courses, coaching, consulting, and more.

We will explain how to create and sell your products and services through Twitter and discuss the best practices and tips for creating landing pages, sales funnels, and payment systems that convert your Twitter followers into customers. We will also provide some tools and resources for creating and selling your products and services through Twitter. Finally, we will share some dos and don'ts for promoting your products and services through your tweets and bio.

How to create and sell your products and services through Twitter.

The first step to selling your products and services through Twitter is to create them. Depending on your niche, skills, and goals, you can create different types of products and services, such as:

Ebooks: Ebooks are digital books that you can write and publish on various topics, such as business, personal development, health, fitness, etc. You can use tools like Canva https://www.canva.com/create/ebooks/, Google Docs **https://docs.google.com/,** or Scrivener **(https://www.literatureandlatte.com/scrivener/overview)** to create and format your ebooks, and platforms like Amazon Kindle Direct Publishing **https://kdp.amazon.com/en_US/,** Gumroad https://gumroad.com/, or Leanpub https://leanpub.com/ to sell them.

Courses: Courses are online learning programs that you can create and sell on various subjects, such as marketing, design, programming, etc. You can use tools like Teachable https://teachable.com/, Thinkific **https://www.thinkific.com/**, or Podia https://www.podia.com/ to create and host your courses, and platforms like Udemy **https://www.udemy.com/**, Skillshare **https://www.skillshare.com/**, or Coursera **https://www.coursera.org/** to sell them.

Coaching: Coaching is a service that you can offer to help your clients achieve their goals, overcome their challenges, or improve their skills, such as life coaching, career coaching, fitness coaching, etc. You can use tools like Calendly https://calendly.com/, Zoom **https://zoom.us/**, or Skype https://www.skype.com/en/ to schedule and conduct your coaching sessions, and platforms like Coach. Me **https://www.coach.me/**, Clarity **https://clarity.fm/**, or Savvy **https://www.savvy.is/** to sell them.

Consulting: Consulting is a service that you can offer to provide your expertise, advice, or solutions to your clients, such as business consulting, legal consulting, financial consulting, etc. You can use tools like Google Meet **https://meet.google.com/**, Slack **https://slack.com/**, or Asana **https://asana.com/** to communicate and collaborate with your clients, and platforms like Upwork https://www.upwork.com/, Fiverr **https://www.fiverr.com/**, or Freelancer https://www.freelancer.com/ o sell them.

These are just some examples of the products and services that you can create and sell through Twitter. You can also create and sell other types of products and services, such as podcasts, webinars, software, apps, etc. The key is to create something that provides value to your target audience, solves their problems, or fulfills their needs or desires.

Once you have created your product or service, the next step is to sell it through Twitter. To do this, you need to create a landing page, a sales funnel, and a payment system for your product or service.

How to create landing pages, sales funnels, and payment systems that convert your Twitter followers into customers.

A landing page is a web page that showcases your product or service and persuades your visitors to take a specific action, such as signing up, buying, or downloading. A sales funnel is a series of steps that guides your visitors from the landing page to the final purchase or conversion. A payment system is a tool that enables you to accept and process payments from your customers.

To create a landing page, a sales funnel, and a payment system for your product or service, you can use tools like Leadpages https://www.leadpages.com/, ClickFunnels **https://www.clickfunnels.com/**, or Stripe **https://stripe.com/**. These tools allow you to create and customize your landing pages, sales funnels, and payment systems without coding or technical skills. They also integrate and with other tools, such as email marketing, analytics, etc.

The best practices and tips for creating landing pages, sales funnels, and payment systems that convert your Twitter followers into customers are:

Know your audience: Before you create your landing page, sales funnel, or payment system, you need to know who your target audience is, what their pain points are, what their goals are, and what motivates them to buy your product or service. You can use tools like Twitter Analytics **https://analytics.twitter.com/**, Google Analytics **https://analytics.google.com**), or SurveyMonkey **https://www.surveymonkey.com/** to collect and analyze data about your audience, such as their demographics, interests, behaviors, etc.

Craft a compelling offer: Your offer is the main reason why your visitors should buy your product or service. It should highlight the benefits, features, and value of your product or service, and how it can solve your visitors' problems or fulfill their needs or desires. You can use tools like CoSchedule Headline Analyzer **https://coschedule.com/headline-analyzer**, Hemingway Editor **http://www.hemingwayapp.com/**, or Grammarly **https://www.grammarly.com/** to craft a clear, concise, and catchy offer that grabs your visitors' attention and curiosity.

Build trust and credibility: Your visitors need to trust you and your product or service before they buy from you. You can build trust and credibility by providing social proof, testimonials, reviews, ratings, guarantees, etc. You can use tools like Trustpilot **https://www.trustpilot.com/**, **Yotpo https://www.yotpo.com/**, or Loox **https://loox.io/** to collect and display social proof, testimonials, reviews, ratings, etc. on your landing page, sales funnel, or payment system.

Create urgency and scarcity: Your visitors need to feel a sense of urgency and scarcity to buy your product or service now, rather than later or never. You can create urgency and scarcity by offering limited-time discounts, bonuses, free trials, etc. You can use tools like Deadline Funne **https://deadlinefunnel.com/**,

[Thrive Ultimatum](https://thrivethemes.com/ultimatum/), or [Evergreen Countdown Timer](https://www.evergreencountdown.com/) to create and display countdown timers, expiring offers, etc. on your landing page, sales funnel, or payment system.

Optimize for conversions: Your landing page, sales funnel, or payment system should be optimized for conversions, meaning that it should be easy, fast, and smooth for your visitors to complete the desired action. You can optimize for conversions by using clear and compelling calls to action, minimizing distractions, simplifying forms, reducing friction, etc. You can use tools like [Unbounce](https://unbounce.com/), [Optimizely](https://www.optimizely.com/), or [Hotjar](https://www.hotjar.com/) to test and improve your landing page, sales funnel, or payment system for conversions.

How to promote your products and services through your tweets and bio.

The final step to selling your products and services through Twitter is to promote them through your tweets and bio. Your tweets and bio are the main ways to attract, engage, and convert your Twitter followers into customers.

To promote your products and services through your tweets and bio, you can use the following dos and don'ts:

Do provide value: Your tweets and bio should provide value to your followers, such as useful information, tips, insights, stories, etc. that are relevant to your niche, product, or service. You can use tools like [Buffer](https://buffer.com/), [Hootsuite](https://hootsuite.com/), or [TweetDeck

https://tweetdeck.twitter.com/ to schedule and manage your tweets, and tools like Bitly **https://bitly.com/**, Rebrandly **https://www.rebrandly.com/**, or TinyURL https://tinyurl.com/ to shorten and track your links.

Do be authentic: Your tweets and bio should reflect your personality, voice, and style, and show your followers who you are, what you do, and why you do it. You can use tools like Twitter Bio Generator https://www.twitterbiogenerator.com/, Bio. Fm **https://bio.fm/**, or Linktree **https://linktr.ee/** to create and optimize your bio, and tools like Namechk **https://namechk.com/**, KnowEm **https://knowem.com/**, or BrandYourself **https://brandyourself.com/** to secure your username and brand across social media platforms.

Do be consistent: Your tweets and bio should be consistent with your niche, product, or service, and align with your brand identity, values, and message. You can use tools like BrandColors **https://brandcolors.net/**, Canva Brand Kit **https://www.canva.com/brand-kit/**, or Tailor Brands **https://www.tailorbrands.com/** to create and maintain your brand identity, colors, fonts, logos, etc.

Don't spam: Your tweets and bio should not spam your followers with excessive, irrelevant, or unsolicited promotions of your product or service. You can use tools like SocialBee **https://socialbee.io/**, MeetEdgar **https://meetedgar.com/**, or SmarterQueue **https://smarterqueue.com/** to create and automate your social media content strategy, and tools like SocialPilot **https://www.socialpilot.co/**, Sprout Social **https://sproutsocial.com/**, or Agorapulse **https://www.agorapulse.com/** to monitor and measure your social media performance and engagement.

Don't be pushy: Your tweets and bio should not be pushy, aggressive, or manipulative in selling your product or service. You can use tools like Loomly **https://www.loomly.com/**, Planable **https://planable.io/**, or CoSchedule **https://coschedule.com/** to plan and preview your tweets and bio, and tools like Grammarly Tone Detector **https://www.grammarly.com/tone**, [Hemingway Editor **http://www.hemingwayapp.com/**, or ProWritingAid **https://prowritingaid.com/** to check and improve your tone, readability, and writing style.

By following these dos and don'ts, you can effectively promote your products and services through your tweets and bio, and turn your Twitter followers into loyal customers.

Affiliate Marketing.

Affiliate marketing is a form of online marketing where you earn commissions by promoting other people's or companies' products or services to your audience. You do this by creating and sharing affiliate links, which are special URLs that track the referrals and sales that you generate. When someone clicks on your affiliate link and makes a purchase or performs a desired action, you get a percentage of the revenue or a fixed amount as a reward.

Affiliate marketing is a popular and effective way to monetize your online presence, especially if you have a blog, a website, a podcast, a YouTube channel, or a large social media following. You can leverage your existing content and audience to recommend products or services that are relevant, useful, and valuable to them, and earn passive income in return.

Types of Affiliate Programs and Networks.

There are many different types of affiliate programs and networks that you can join, depending on your niche, goals, and preferences. Some examples of the ones that are often used and beneficial are:

Amazon Associates: This is one of the largest and most popular affiliate programs in the world, as it allows you to promote any product that is sold on Amazon.com, the e-commerce giant. You can earn up to 10% commission on each sale, depending on the product category and the volume of sales you generate. You can also earn commissions from other products that the customer buys within 24 hours of clicking on your link, even if they are not the ones you promoted.

ClickBank: This is a leading marketplace for digital products, such as e-books, courses, software, etc. You can find products in various niches, such as health, fitness, business, education, etc. You can earn up to 75% commission on each sale, depending on the product and the vendor. You can also earn recurring commissions from subscription-based products or upsells.

ShareASale: This is a large and reputable affiliate network that connects you with thousands of merchants and brands across different industries and categories. You can find products and services in niches such as fashion, beauty, home, travel, etc. You can earn commissions ranging from 1% to 50% or more, depending on the merchant and the product. You can also earn bonuses, incentives, and performance-based rewards from some merchants.

These are just some examples of the many affiliate programs and networks that are available online. You can also find niche-specific or product-specific programs that suit your needs and interests. For example, if you are a travel blogger, you can join affiliate programs from airlines, hotels, booking sites, travel agencies, etc. If you are a tech enthusiast, you can join affiliate programs from software companies, gadget manufacturers, online platforms, etc.

Best Practices and Tips for Finding and Joining Affiliate Programs and Networks.

Finding and joining affiliate programs and networks is not difficult, but it requires some research and planning. Here is some helpful advice and best practices that can support you:

Know your audience: The first and most important step is to understand your audience, their needs, problems, desires, preferences, and behaviors. You need to know what kind of products or services they are looking for, what they are willing to pay for, and what they trust and value. This will help you find and promote products or services that are relevant, useful, and valuable to them, and that will solve their pain points or enhance their lives.

Know your niche: The second step is to identify your niche or the specific topic or category that you focus on with your content and audience. You need to know what kind of products or services are available and popular in your niche, what are the trends and opportunities, and what are the gaps and challenges. This will help you find and promote products or services that are aligned with your niche, and that will differentiate you from your competitors.

Know your goals: The third step is to define your goals, or what you want to achieve with affiliate marketing. You need to know how much money you want to make, how much time and effort you want to invest, and how you want to measure your success. This will help you find and promote products or services that are compatible with your goals, and that will motivate you to work hard and smart.

Research and compare: The fourth step is to research and compare different affiliate programs and networks that are relevant to your audience, niche, and goals. You need to know the details and requirements of each program or network, such as the commission rates, payment methods, cookie duration, tracking system, support, etc. You also need to know the quality and reputation of the products or services, the conversion rates, the customer reviews, the refund policy, etc. This will help you find and promote products or services that are reliable, profitable, and trustworthy.

Apply and join: The fifth step is to apply and join the affiliate programs or networks that you have selected. You need to follow the instructions and guidelines of each program or network, such as filling out an application form, providing your personal and payment information, agreeing to the terms and conditions, etc. You also need to wait for the approval or rejection of your application, which may take from a few minutes to a few days, depending on the program or network. Once you are approved, you can access your affiliate dashboard, where you can find and generate your affiliate links, banners, widgets, etc.

Tools and Resources for Creating and Managing Affiliate Links and Tracking Your Commissions:

Creating and managing affiliate links and tracking your commissions are essential tasks for affiliate marketing. You need to make sure that your links are working properly, that they are easy to use and share, and that they are compliant with the rules and regulations of the affiliate programs or networks and the platforms that you use. You also need to monitor and analyze your performance, such as the number of clicks, sales, conversions, commissions, etc. This will help you optimize your strategy, improve your results, and grow your income.

Many tools and resources can help you with these tasks, such as: Link shorteners: These are services that allow you to shorten and customize your affiliate links, making them more user-friendly and attractive. Some examples are **Bitly**, **TinyURL**, **Rebrandly**, etc. Some of these services also provide analytics and tracking features, such as the number of clicks, referrals, sources, locations, etc.

Link cloakers: These are services that allow you to hide and protect your affiliate links, making them more secure and professional. Some examples are **Pretty Links, ThirstyAffiliates, WP Cloaker**, etc. Some of these services also provide features such as keyword replacement, link redirection, link grouping, etc.

Link trackers: These are services that allow you to track and measure your affiliate links, making them more effective and profitable. Some examples are **ClickMeter, Voluum, ClickMagick**, etc. These services provide features such as real-time reporting, conversion tracking, split testing, link rotators, etc.

Affiliate plugins: These are plugins that allow you to create and manage your affiliate links and banners, making them more convenient and integrated. Some examples are **Easy Affiliate Links, AffiliateWP, WP Affiliate Manager**, etc. These plugins provide features such as link insertion, link management, link display, link backup, etc.

Affiliate dashboards: These are dashboards that allow you to access and manage your affiliate accounts and commissions, making them more centralized and organized. Some examples are **Affilorama, Affluent, AffJet**, etc. These dashboards provide features such as account integration, commission aggregation, commission reporting, commission alerts, etc.

Dos and Don'ts for Posting Affiliate Links and Promoting Affiliate Products and Services Through Your Tweets and Bio:

Posting affiliate links and promoting affiliate products and services through your tweets and bio are effective ways to reach and engage your audience, generate traffic, and increase conversions. However, you need to follow some dos and don'ts to ensure that you are doing it right, ethically, and legally. Here are some of them:

Do disclose your affiliate relationship and comply with the FTC guidelines and the terms and conditions of the affiliate programs or networks and the platforms that you use. You need to inform your audience that you are using affiliate links and that you may earn commissions from them, and you need to use clear and conspicuous disclosure statements, such as #ad, #sponsored, #affiliate, etc.

Don't spam your audience with too many irrelevant affiliate links and promotions. You need to respect your audience's time and attention, and you need to provide value and quality to them. You need to use affiliate links and promotions sparingly and strategically, and you need to make sure that they are relevant, useful, and valuable to your audience and niche.

To provide honest and helpful reviews and recommendations of the affiliate products and services that you promote. You need to build trust and credibility with your audience, and you need to help them make informed and smart decisions. You need to share your personal experience, opinion, and feedback on the affiliate products and services, and you need to highlight their benefits, features, and drawbacks.

Don't mislead or deceive your audience with false or exaggerated claims or promises of the affiliate products and services that you promote. You need to be truthful and transparent with your audience, and you need to avoid any potential conflicts of interest or legal issues. You need to avoid making any guarantees, warranties, or testimonials that are not supported by evidence or facts, and you need to avoid any claims that violate the terms and conditions or the policies of the affiliate program or network or the platform that you use.

Do engage and interact with your audience and provide value and support to them. You need to create and maintain a relationship with your audience, and you need to provide them with useful and relevant information, tips, advice, resources, etc. You need to answer their questions, address their concerns, solicit their feedback, thank them for their support, etc.

Don't be pushy or salesy with your affiliate links and promotions. You need to respect your audience's choices and preferences, and you need to avoid any pressure or manipulation tactics. You need to avoid using any aggressive or annoying language, such as "buy now", "don't miss this opportunity", "limited time offer", etc. You need to avoid using any pop-ups, banners, or widgets that interfere with your content or user experience.

These are some of the dos and don'ts for posting affiliate links and promoting affiliate products and services through your tweets and bio. By following these guidelines, you can increase your chances of success and income with affiliate marketing, while also maintaining your reputation and integrity.

Creator Subscriptions.

As a creator on Twitter, you have the opportunity to monetize your content and build a loyal fan base through creator subscriptions. Creator subscriptions are a way for you to offer exclusive content and perks to your followers who pay a monthly fee to support you.

What are creator subscriptions and how do they work?
What are the different types of creator subscriptions and how to choose the best one for you?
What are the best practices and tips for launching and growing your creator subscriptions and offering value to your paid subscribers?
What are some tools and resources for creating and managing your creator subscriptions and delivering your exclusive content and perks?
What are some dos and don'ts for posting and promoting your creator subscriptions through your tweets and bio?

What are creator subscriptions and how do they work?

Creator subscriptions are a form of direct-to-fan monetization that allows you to charge your followers a monthly fee in exchange for access to exclusive content and perks that you create and deliver. This can include things like:

Behind-the-scenes videos, photos, or podcasts.
Early access to your new projects, products, or services.
Live Q&A sessions, polls, or surveys.
Shout-outs, acknowledgments, or thank-you messages.
Discounts, coupons, or giveaways.
Custom emojis, badges, or stickers

Private chats, groups, or communities.

Creator subscriptions can help you generate a steady and recurring income from your content, as well as deepen your relationship with your most engaged and loyal fans. You can also use creator subscriptions to test new ideas, get feedback, and validate your market before launching a bigger project or product.

To start offering creator subscriptions, you need to choose a platform or service that enables you to create and manage your subscription program. There are many options available, each with its features, benefits, and drawbacks. We will discuss some of the most popular ones in the next section.

What are the different types of creator subscriptions and how to choose the best one for you?

There are many types of creator subscriptions that you can choose from, depending on your goals, preferences, and audience. Here are some of the most common ones:

Super Follows: Super Follows is a feature that Twitter is currently testing and rolling out to select users. It allows you to offer exclusive content and perks to your followers who pay a monthly fee of $2.99, $4.99, or $9.99. You can set up your Super Follows page within the Twitter app, and your subscribers can access your exclusive content and perks through a separate tab on your profile. You can also interact with your subscribers through a dedicated Super Follows feed. Twitter takes a 3% cut of your revenue until you reach $50,000 in lifetime earnings, after which it increases to 20%.

Patreon: Patreon is one of the most popular and established platforms for creator subscriptions. It allows you to create multiple tiers of membership, each with its price and benefits. You can offer exclusive content and perks through Patreon's website, app, or integrations with other platforms like Discord, YouTube, or WordPress. You can also interact with your patrons through posts, messages, or live streams. Patreon takes a 5%, 8%, or 12% cut of your revenue, depending on your plan, plus payment processing fees.

Substack: Substack is a platform that focuses on email newsletters. It allows you to create a free or paid newsletter that you can send to your subscribers on a regular or occasional basis. You can offer exclusive content and perks through your newsletter, such as access to archives, comments, or podcasts. You can also interact with your subscribers through replies, discussions, or polls. Substack takes a 10% cut of your revenue, plus payment processing fees.

Other options: There are many other options for creator subscriptions, such as OnlyFans, Gumroad, Memberful, Podia, Buy Me a Coffee, and more. Each of these platforms has its features, benefits, and drawbacks, and you should do your research and compare them before choosing the best one for you.

Some of the factors that you should consider when choosing a platform for your creator subscriptions are:

The size, demographics, and preferences of your audience.
The type, format, and frequency of your content and perks.
The level of control, customization, and integration that you want.
The fees, commissions, and taxes that you have to pay.
The support, community, and resources that you can access.

What are the best practices and tips for launching and growing your creator subscriptions and offering value to your paid subscribers?

Launching and growing your creator subscriptions is not an easy task. It requires a lot of planning, preparation, and promotion. These are some useful tips and best practices that can assist you:

Define your value proposition: You need to communicate what your creator subscriptions are, why they are worth paying for, and what your subscribers can expect from you. You need to highlight the benefits and outcomes that your content and perks can provide, and how they can solve a problem, fulfill a need, or satisfy a desire for your audience. You need to also differentiate yourself from other creators and show what makes you unique and valuable.

Know your audience: You need to understand who your ideal subscribers are, what they want, what they need, and what they are willing to pay for. You need to create content and perks that match their interests, preferences, and expectations. You need to also segment your audience and offer different tiers of membership, each with its price and benefits, to cater to different levels of engagement and willingness to pay.

Create a launch plan: You need to create a launch plan that outlines your goals, strategies, and tactics for launching your creator subscriptions. You need to decide when, where, and how you will announce your creator subscriptions, and how you will generate interest, excitement, and urgency among your potential subscribers. You need to also prepare your content and perks in advance, and make sure that they are ready to be delivered on time and with quality.

Promote your creator subscriptions: You need to promote your creator subscriptions through your tweets and bio, as well as other channels and platforms that you use. You need to create compelling and consistent messages that showcase your value proposition, highlight your content and perks, and invite your followers to join your subscription program. You need to also leverage social proof, testimonials, and referrals from your existing subscribers, and offer incentives, discounts, or bonuses for signing up or inviting others.

Engage your subscribers: You need to engage your subscribers regularly and make them feel valued, appreciated, and connected. You need to deliver your content and perks as promised and exceed their expectations. You need to also interact with your subscribers through feedback, questions, polls, surveys, live streams, or chats. You need to also acknowledge, thank, and reward your subscribers for their support, and ask them for reviews, ratings, or recommendations.

What are some tools and resources for creating and managing your creator subscriptions and delivering your exclusive content and perks?

Creating and managing your creator subscriptions and delivering your exclusive content and perks can be challenging and time-consuming. Fortunately, many tools and resources can help you with these tasks. Here are some of them:

Twitter tools: Twitter offers some tools that can help you with your creator subscriptions, such as:
Twitter Media Studio: This is a dashboard that allows you to upload, manage, and schedule your media content, such as

photos, videos, GIFs, or polls. You can also access analytics and insights on your media performance and engagement.

Twitter Spaces: This is a feature that allows you to create and host live audio conversations with your followers or subscribers. You can also invite guests, co-hosts, or speakers, and moderate the discussion.

Twitter Fleets: This is a feature that allows you to share ephemeral stories that disappear after 24 hours. You can use this to share behind-the-scenes, teasers, or previews of your exclusive content and perks.

Content creation tools: Many tools can help you create your exclusive content and perks, such as:

Canva: This is a graphic design tool that allows you to create and edit images, logos, flyers, posters, banners, or infographics. You can also access templates, icons, fonts, or stock photos.

Anchor: This is a podcasting tool that allows you to record, edit, and distribute your podcasts. You can also access music, sound effects, or analytics.

Loom: This is a video recording tool that allows you to record your screen, webcam, or voice. You can also edit, caption, or share your videos.

Content delivery tools: Many tools can help you deliver your exclusive content and perks, such as:

Discord: This is a chat platform that allows you to create and manage your private chats, groups, or communities. You can also integrate it with other platforms like Patreon, Twitch, or YouTube.

Mailchimp: This is an email marketing tool that allows you to create and send your newsletters. You can also segment, personalize, or automate your emails, and access analytics and insights.

Gumroad: This is a digital product platform that allows you to sell and deliver your digital products, such as ebooks, courses, or software. You can also set up pay-what-you-want, subscriptions, or memberships.

Content management tools: Many tools can help you manage your creator subscriptions and track your performance, such as:
Google Analytics: This is a web analytics tool that allows you to measure your website traffic, conversions, and user behavior. You can also set up goals, events, or custom reports.
Stripe: This is a payment processing tool that allows you to accept and manage payments from your subscribers. You can also access invoices, receipts, or refunds.
Airtable: This is a spreadsheet-database hybrid tool that allows you to organize and store your data, such as your subscriber list, content calendar, or feedback. You can also create views, forms, or charts.

What are some dos and don'ts for posting and promoting your creator subscriptions through your tweets and bio?

Posting and promoting your creator subscriptions through your tweets and bio is an essential part of growing your audience and revenue. However, it requires carefulness and strategy from you. Follow these guidelines on what to do and what to avoid:

Do: Use your bio to showcase your value proposition, your content and perks, and your call to action. You can also use emojis, hashtags, or links to make it more appealing and clickable.

Don't: Use your bio to spam, beg, or pressure your followers to join your creator subscriptions. You should also avoid using misleading, false, or exaggerated claims or promises.

Do: Use your tweets to share valuable, relevant, and engaging content that showcases your expertise, personality, and style. You can also use media, polls, or fleets to make it more interactive and visual.

Don't: Use your tweets to constantly pitch, sell, or promote your creator subscriptions. You should also avoid using clickbait, hype, or manipulation tactics to get attention or conversions.

Do: Use your tweets to tease, preview, or highlight your exclusive content and perks, and invite your followers to join your creator subscriptions to access them. You can also use testimonials, referrals, or incentives to encourage them to sign up or share.

Don't: Use your tweets to reveal, leak, or spoil your exclusive content and perks, and undermine the value of your creator subscriptions. You should also avoid using guilt, shame, or fear to motivate them to join or stay.

X Ads Revenue Sharing Program.

X Ads Revenue Sharing Program is a new initiative by X that allows creators to earn a share of the ad revenue generated from their posts. The program is designed to incentivize creators to post content that encourages conversation and engagement. We will explain what X Ads Revenue Sharing Program is and how it works, how to make money from it, and the process of doing it including payment mode, the eligibility criteria and application process for joining the program, the best practices and tips for optimizing your tweets and maximizing your ad revenue share, some tools and resources for tracking and analyzing your ad performance and earnings, and some dos and don'ts for posting and participating in the program.

What is the X Ads Revenue Sharing Program and how does it work?

X Ads Revenue Sharing Program is a way for creators to monetize their organic impressions of ads displayed in replies to their content on X. This means that whenever a verified user sees an ad in the reply section of a tweet posted by a creator who is enrolled in the program, the creator will receive a percentage of the ad revenue. This is part of X's effort to help people earn a living directly on X and to reward creators for their contribution to the platform. Creators can set up Ads Revenue Sharing and Creator Subscriptions independently, and they can choose to participate in both or either of them.

The amount of revenue that a creator can earn from the program depends on several factors, such as the number of impressions, the type and quality of the ads, the location and demographics of the audience, and the market rates. X does not disclose the exact percentage of the revenue share, but it is reported to be competitive with other platforms. X pays out the revenue share to creators every month, as long as they have generated more than USD 10 in a given month. X may modify or cancel the program at any time in its sole discretion, and it reserves the right to accept or revoke the participation of any creator in the program.

The eligibility criteria for the program:

To make money from the X Ads Revenue Sharing Program, a creator needs to meet the eligibility criteria, apply for the program, set up a Stripe account, post content that generates replies and impressions, and comply with the program terms and conditions.

The eligibility criteria for the program are:

Join X Premium or Verified Organizations as a subscriber
Have at least 15M organic impressions on your cumulative posts within the last 3 months
Have at least 500 followers

The application process for the program is:
Access the Monetization section in the settings menu on X
Click on **Join and set payouts** if you want to share ad revenue.
Agree to the program terms and conditions, which include the Creator Monetization Standards and the X Rules
Create or link a Stripe account, which is the payment processor for the program
Start posting content and earning revenue share

The payment mode for the program is:

X transfers the revenue share to the creator's Stripe account every month

The creator can transfer the funds from Stripe to their external bank account

The creator is responsible for any taxes, fees, or charges associated with the payments

Best practices and tips for optimizing your tweets and maximizing your ad revenue share:

To optimize your tweets and maximize your ad revenue share, here are some best practices and tips that you can follow:

Post content that is relevant, engaging, and original. Avoid posting spam, low-quality, or duplicated content that may violate the program terms and conditions or the X Rules.

Post content that sparks conversation and encourages replies from verified users. Use questions, polls, challenges, opinions, or other formats that invite interaction and feedback. The more replies your content receives, the more ads will be displayed and the more revenue you will earn.

Post content that appeals to a broad and diverse audience. The more impressions your content receives, the more revenue you will earn. Try to reach out to different segments of your followers and potential followers, and use hashtags, keywords, or trends to increase your visibility and discoverability.

Post content that is suitable for ads. Avoid posting content that is sensitive, controversial, or offensive, as this may limit the types and quality of ads that can be shown on your content. Also, avoid posting content that directly promotes or endorses a product, service, or brand, as this may conflict with the ads that are shown on your content.

Post content regularly and consistently. Maintain a steady and frequent posting schedule that keeps your followers engaged and interested. Experiment with different times, days, and frequencies to find the optimal posting pattern for your audience and niche.

Tools and resources for tracking and analyzing your ad performance and earnings:

To track and analyze your ad performance and earnings, you can use some tools and resources that are available on X or externally. Some of them are:

X Analytics: This is the official tool that X provides to creators to monitor their ad revenue share and other metrics, such as impressions, engagements, followers, and profile visits. You can access X Analytics from the Monetization section in the settings menu on X, or the analytics.x.com website. You can also download your data as a CSV file for further analysis.

Stripe Dashboard: This is the tool that Stripe provides to creators to manage their payments and payouts from X. You can access Stripe Dashboard from the Monetization section in the settings menu on X, or from the stripe.com website. You can also view your transaction history, balance, and invoices, and set up your bank account details and tax information.

Third-party tools: There are also some third-party tools that you can use to track and analyze your ad performance and earnings, such as Social Blade, Hype Auditor, or Influencer Marketing Hub. These tools may offer additional features or insights that are not available on X Analytics or Stripe Dashboard, such as estimated earnings, engagement rate, audience quality, or competitor analysis. However, you should be careful when using these tools, as they may not be accurate, reliable, or secure, and they may require you to share your personal or account information.

Some dos and don'ts for posting and participating in the program:

To ensure a positive and successful experience with X Ads Revenue Sharing Program, here are some dos and don'ts that you should follow:

Do read and understand the program terms and conditions, the Creator Monetization Standards, and the X Rules, and comply with them at all times. These are the guidelines and policies that govern your participation in the program, and they are designed to protect you, your audience, and X from any harm or abuse.

Do respect and appreciate your followers and other users on X. They are the ones who support you and enable you to earn revenue from the program. Engage with them in a friendly and constructive manner, and acknowledge their feedback and suggestions. Avoid being rude, abusive, or disrespectful to anyone on X, and report any inappropriate or harmful behavior that you encounter.

Be authentic and transparent about your content and your participation in the program. Share your own original and creative content that reflects your personality and passion. Disclose any affiliations, partnerships, or sponsorships that you have with any products, services, or brands that you mention or feature in your content. Do not mislead, deceive, or manipulate your followers or other users on X, and do not use any fraudulent or unethical methods to increase your impressions, replies, or revenue.

Don't expect to make a lot of money quickly or easily from the program. The program is not a get-rich-quick scheme, and it requires a lot of time, effort, and dedication to build and maintain a loyal and engaged audience and to create and post quality and relevant content. The amount of revenue that you can earn from the program depends on many factors, and it may vary from month to month. Don't rely solely on the program as your main or only source of income, and don't compare yourself with other creators who may have different results or circumstances.

Don't spam, harass, or annoy your followers or other users on X with your content or your participation in the program. Don't post too much or too often, or post irrelevant or repetitive content that may clutter or disrupt the X experience. Don't beg, solicit, or pressure your followers or other users to reply to your content or to click on the ads that are shown on your content. Don't use bots, scripts, or other automated or artificial means to generate impressions, replies, or revenue.

Twitter is not only a powerful platform for sharing information, opinions, and stories, but also a lucrative source of income for many users. In this chapter, we have explored and evaluated the various income opportunities and models available on Twitter, and how you can leverage them to monetize your online presence and influence.

We have discussed how you can find and partner with brands, businesses, and platforms that offer paid opportunities for Twitter users, such as sponsored tweets, influencer campaigns, and ambassador programs. We have also provided tips and best practices for creating and posting sponsored tweets that promote products, services, or causes authentically and ethically, without compromising your credibility and reputation.

We have also shown how you can sell your products and services through Twitter by creating landing pages, sales funnels, and payment systems that convert your followers into customers. We have explained how you can use Twitter to showcase your expertise, skills, and solutions, and to generate leads, traffic, and sales for your offerings.

Moreover, we have introduced the concept of affiliate marketing and how you can earn commissions by promoting other people's products and services through your tweets and bio. We have outlined the steps and strategies for finding and joining affiliate programs, choosing and recommending relevant and quality products and services, and creating effective and engaging affiliate tweets.

Furthermore, we have explored the option of launching creator subscriptions and offering exclusive content and perks to your paid subscribers. We have discussed the benefits and challenges of creating a subscription-based model, and how you can use

Twitter to build and grow a loyal and engaged fan base that is willing to pay for your content.

Finally, we have presented the X Ads Revenue Sharing Program, a new and innovative way of earning a share of the ad revenue generated by your tweets. We have explained how the program works, how you can join and qualify, and how you can optimize your tweets to increase your ad revenue potential.

Twitter offers a variety of income opportunities and models for users who want to monetize their online presence and influence. By exploring and evaluating these options, and applying the tips and best practices we have shared, you can create and implement a successful and sustainable income strategy that suits your goals, niche, and audience.

Chapter Six

Avoiding Common Mistakes.

Twitter is a powerful and popular platform that offers many income opportunities for content creators, influencers, marketers, and entrepreneurs. However, making money on Twitter is more challenging than it may seem. Many common mistakes can jeopardize your success, damage your reputation, or even get you banned from the platform. We will discuss some of the most important pitfalls to avoid and how to overcome them if you encounter them. We will cover the following topics:

Understanding and complying with the Twitter rules and policies that govern the use of the platform and the income opportunities. We will explain the main guidelines and regulations you must follow to avoid violating the terms of service, the community standards, and the advertising policies of Twitter and its partners. We will also provide some tips and best practices on how to stay compliant and avoid penalties, suspensions, or legal actions.

Balancing your promotional and non-promotional content to avoid annoying or alienating your followers. We will explore the optimal ratio and frequency of posting promotional content versus non-promotional content, and how to create value and engagement for your audience. We will also show you how to avoid spamming, overselling, or misleading your followers with your promotional messages, and how to maintain trust and authenticity with your audience.

Protecting your reputation and credibility by disclosing your partnerships, endorsements, and affiliations. We will discuss the ethical and legal implications of disclosing your relationships with brands, sponsors, affiliates, or other entities that you promote or collaborate with on Twitter. We will also provide some examples and recommendations on how to disclose your partnerships, endorsements, and affiliations clearly and transparently, and how to comply with the relevant laws and regulations in your jurisdiction.

Handling negative feedback, criticism, and complaints professionally and respectfully. We will examine the common sources and types of negative feedback, criticism, and complaints that you may receive on Twitter, and how to respond to them effectively and constructively. We will also teach you how to deal with trolls, haters, and cyber bullies, and how to protect your mental health and well-being from the stress and pressure of online negativity.

Recovering from setbacks and failures and learning from your mistakes. We will share some stories and lessons from successful Twitter income earners who faced challenges, difficulties, and failures in their journey, and how they overcame them and learned from them. We will also provide some strategies and tips on how to bounce back from setbacks and failures and use them as opportunities for growth and improvement.

By the end of this chapter, you will have a better understanding of the common mistakes that can hinder your Twitter income potential, and how to avoid or overcome them. You will also have the skills and confidence to handle any challenges or difficulties that may arise in your Twitter income journey, and to learn from your mistakes and grow from them.

Understand and Comply with the Twitter Rules and Policies.

Twitter is a powerful platform that allows you to connect with millions of people around the world, share your thoughts and opinions, and earn income from various sources. However, with great power comes great responsibility. To ensure that Twitter remains a safe, respectful, and trustworthy place for everyone, you need to follow the rules and policies that govern the use of the platform and the income opportunities. We will explain why this is important, what are some of the key rules and policies you need to be aware of, how to find and understand them, and what are the possible consequences of violating them.

Why is it important to follow the Twitter rules and policies?

Following Twitter rules and policies is not only a matter of compliance but also a matter of ethics and reputation. By adhering to the standards and expectations set by Twitter, you are showing respect and consideration for your fellow users, your audience, your partners, and the platform itself. You are also protecting yourself from legal, financial, and reputational risks that may arise from engaging in prohibited or inappropriate activities. Moreover, you are enhancing your credibility and trustworthiness as a content creator, influencer, or advertiser, which can help you attract and retain more followers, customers, and partners, and ultimately increase your income potential.

What are some of the Twitter rules and policies that are relevant to Twitter income?

Many rules and policies apply to different aspects of using Twitter, such as content, accounts, advertising, and partner policies. You should familiarize yourself with all of them, but here are some of the most relevant ones for Twitter income:

Content policies: These policies regulate what kind of content you can or cannot post, share, or promote on Twitter, such as prohibited content (e.g., illegal, violent, hateful, abusive, misleading, etc.), sensitive content (e.g., graphic, adult, medical, etc.), spam (e.g., unsolicited, repetitive, deceptive, etc.), and intellectual property (e.g., copyright, trademark, etc.). You should always create and share content that is original, authentic, accurate, respectful, and appropriate for your audience and the platform.

Account policies: These policies regulate how you can or cannot use your Twitter account, such as impersonation (e.g., pretending to be someone else), multiple accounts (e.g., creating or using more than one account for the same purpose), verification (e.g., applying for or displaying the blue badge), and account security (e.g., protecting your password, enabling two-factor authentication, etc.). You should always use your account in a way that is consistent with your identity, purpose, and integrity, and avoid any actions that may compromise your account or others'.

Advertising policies: These policies regulate how you can or cannot advertise or monetize your content or account on Twitter, such as eligibility (e.g., meeting the minimum requirements for age, location, followers, etc.), transparency (e.g., disclosing your relationship with the advertiser or sponsor), disclosure (e.g., using the appropriate labels or hashtags to indicate paid or promotional content), and quality (e.g., ensuring that your ads or sponsored content are relevant, accurate, and compliant with the content policies). You should always follow the best practices and guidelines for advertising or monetizing your content or account on Twitter, and respect the rights and preferences of your audience and the platform.

Partner policies: These policies regulate how you can or cannot partner with third-party platforms, services, or programs that offer income opportunities on Twitter, such as terms and conditions (e.g., agreeing to and abiding by the rules and obligations of the partnership), guidelines (e.g., following the recommendations and standards of the partner), best practices (e.g., optimizing your content or account for the partner's goals and metrics), and feedback (e.g., responding to and implementing the suggestions or corrections from the partner). You should always choose your partners carefully and wisely, and maintain a professional and mutually beneficial relationship with them.

How to find and understand the Twitter rules and policies?
The Twitter rules and policies are available on the Twitter website, under the Help Center **https://help.twitter.com/en** section. You can access them by clicking on the Rules and policies **https://help.twitter.com/en/rules-and-policies** link, which will take you to a page that lists and explains the various policies that apply to different topics and scenarios. You can also use the search function or the navigation menu to find the specific policy that you are looking for. You should read and understand the rules and policies carefully and thoroughly, and check them regularly for any updates or changes. If you have any questions or doubts about the rules and policies, you can contact Twitter support or consult a legal or professional expert for clarification or advice.

What are the consequences of violating Twitter rules and policies?

Violating the Twitter rules and policies can result in serious and negative consequences, such as:

Account suspension or termination: This means that your account will be temporarily or permanently disabled, and you will lose access to your content, followers, and income sources. This can happen if you repeatedly or severely violate the rules and policies, or if your account poses a significant risk or harm to the platform or the users.

Content removal or restriction: This means that your content will be deleted or limited in its visibility, reach, or functionality. This can happen if your content violates the rules and policies, or if your content receives complaints or reports from the users or the authorities.

Advertising rejection or suspension: This means that your ads or sponsored content will be rejected or suspended from running or displaying on Twitter. This can happen if your ads or sponsored content violate the rules and policies, or if your ads or sponsored content perform poorly or receive negative feedback from the users or the platform.

Partner termination or penalty: This means that your partnership with a third-party platform, service, or program will be terminated or penalized. This can happen if you violate the terms and conditions, guidelines, or best practices of the partner, or if you fail to meet the expectations or requirements of the partner.

Balance Your Promotional and Non-Promotional Content.

If you are using Twitter for business or personal branding purposes, you might want to promote your products, services, or achievements to your followers. However, if you only post promotional content, you might end up annoying or alienating your followers, who might perceive you as spammy, self-centered, or boring. Therefore, it is important to balance your promotional and non-promotional content to maintain a positive and engaging relationship with your audience.

What are Promotional and Non-Promotional Content?
Promotional content is any content that directly or indirectly advertises or sells something to your followers. For example, promotional content can include:

Sponsored posts: These are posts that you get paid to publish by a brand or a company. For example, you might post a picture of yourself wearing a sponsored outfit or using a sponsored product, and tag the brand or company in your post.

Affiliate links: These are links that you share with your followers that direct them to a product or service that you recommend or endorse. For example, you might share a link to a book that you enjoyed reading, and earn a commission if your followers buy the book through your link.

Product reviews: These are posts that you write or record to give your honest opinion or feedback on a product or service that you have used or tried. For example, you might post a video of yourself reviewing a new gadget or app, and rate it on a scale of 1 to 5 stars.

Announcements: These are posts that you use to inform your followers about your latest news, updates, or achievements. For example, you might post a tweet to announce that you have launched a new website, podcast, or course, and invite your followers to check it out.

Non-promotional content is any content that does not directly or indirectly advertise or sell something to your followers. For example, non-promotional content can include:

Personal stories: These are posts that you use to share your personal experiences, insights, or lessons learned with your followers. For example, you might post a tweet to share how you overcame a challenge, learned a new skill, or achieved a goal.

Opinions: These are posts that you use to express your views, thoughts, or feelings on a topic that interests you or your followers. For example, you might post a tweet to share your opinion on a current event, a trending topic, or a controversial issue.

Tips: These are posts that you use to offer your followers some useful advice, guidance, or suggestions on a topic that relates to your niche or industry. For example, you might post a tweet to share a tip on how to improve your productivity, creativity, or well-being.

Questions: These are posts that you use to ask your followers a question, either to solicit their feedback, opinions, or ideas or to start a conversation or a debate. For example, you might post a tweet to ask your followers what they think about a new trend, a new product, or a new policy.

Humor: These are posts that you use to make your followers laugh, smile, or feel amused by your witty, funny, or sarcastic remarks. For example, you might post a tweet to make a joke, a pun, or a meme about something that happened to you, something that you saw, or something that you heard.

How to Balance Your Promotional and Non-Promotional Content?

Balancing your promotional and non-promotional content is not a fixed or exact science, but rather an art that requires some trial and error, experimentation, and testing. However, here are some general tips and best practices that you can follow to achieve a good balance:

Know your audience and their preferences: The first and foremost tip is to know who your followers are, what they want, and what they expect from you. You can use tools like Twitter Analytics to get insights into your followers' demographics, interests, behaviors, and engagement patterns. You can also use polls, surveys, or direct messages to ask your followers what kind of content they like, dislike, or want to see more or less of. By knowing your audience and their preferences, you can tailor your content to suit their needs and wants, and avoid posting content that might annoy or bore them.

Provide value and relevance to your followers: The second tip is to provide value and relevance to your followers with every post that you publish. Whether you post promotional or non-promotional content, you should always aim to offer your followers something that benefits them, educates them, entertains them, or inspires them. You should also make sure that your content is relevant to your niche or industry, and that it aligns with your brand identity, voice, and message. By providing value and relevance to your followers, you can increase your credibility, authority, and trustworthiness, and encourage your followers to engage with your content and take action on your offers.

Be authentic and transparent: The third tip is to be authentic and transparent with your followers and avoid being deceptive, misleading, or dishonest. You should always disclose when you post promotional content, such as sponsored posts or affiliate links, and follow the rules and regulations of Twitter and the Federal Trade Commission (FTC). You should also be honest and genuine when you post non-promotional content and avoid pretending to be someone or something that you are not. By being authentic and transparent with your followers, you can build a loyal, supportive, and respectful community, and avoid losing your followers' trust or respect.

Use hashtags, mentions, and keywords strategically: The fourth tip is to use hashtags, mentions, and keywords strategically to optimize your content for visibility, reach, and engagement. You can use hashtags to categorize your content, join relevant conversations, or create your trends. You can use mentions to tag other users, brands, or organizations that are related to your content, or to give credit, appreciation, or recognition. You can use keywords to make your content searchable, discoverable, or relevant to your niche or industry. However, you should avoid overusing or abusing hashtags, mentions, or keywords, as this might make your content look spammy, cluttered, or irrelevant, and lower your content quality and performance.

Experiment and test different types of content and formats: The fifth and final tip is to experiment and test different types of content and formats to find out what works best for you and your followers. You can try different combinations of promotional and non-promotional content, such as 80/20, 70/30, or 60/40, and see how your followers respond and react. You can also try different formats of content, such as text, images, videos, or live streams, and see how your followers engage and interact.

By experimenting and testing different types of content and formats, you can find your optimal balance, and improve your content quality and effectiveness.

Protect Your Reputation and Credibility.

As a Twitter user, you may have the opportunity to collaborate with brands, partners, or other influencers to create and share content with your audience. This can be a great way to grow your reach, earn income, and provide value to your followers. However, it also comes with some responsibilities and risks that you need to be aware of.

One of the most important aspects of creating and sharing content on Twitter is to protect your reputation and credibility by disclosing your partnerships, endorsements, and affiliations. This means that you need to inform your audience about any relationship or connection that you have with the entities or products that you mention or promote in your content. This is not only a matter of honesty and transparency, but also a legal requirement in many jurisdictions.

Why is disclosure important?

Disclosure is important for several reasons:

It helps you to build trust and loyalty with your audience. By being upfront and clear about your relationships, you show that you respect your followers and value their opinions. You also avoid misleading them or creating false impressions about your content.

It helps you to comply with the laws and regulations that apply to your content. Depending on where you and your audience are located, you may be subject to different rules and guidelines that govern how you should disclose your partnerships, endorsements, and affiliations. For example, in the United States, the Federal Trade Commission (FTC) has issued guidelines **https://www.ftc.gov/tips-advice/business-center/guidance/ftcs-**

endorsement-guides-what-people-are-asking on how to properly endorse products or services on social media platforms, such as Twitter. Failing to follow these guidelines could result in legal action or penalties from the FTC or other authorities.

It helps you to avoid negative consequences for your reputation and credibility. If you do not disclose your relationships, you may face backlash from your audience, the media, or the public. You may also damage your reputation and credibility as a content creator, and lose the trust and respect of your followers, partners, and peers.

What are the types of disclosures that you must make?
The types of disclosures that you need to make depend on the nature and extent of your relationship with the entities or products that you mention or promote in your content. Here are some common examples of the types of disclosures that Twitter users need to make:

Paid or sponsored content: This is when you receive money or other compensation (such as free products, services, or trips) in exchange for creating or sharing content that features or promotes a brand, partner, or product. For example, if you are paid by a clothing company to post a tweet with a picture of yourself wearing their clothes and a link to their website, you need to disclose that this is a paid or sponsored content.

Affiliate or referral links: This is when you include a link in your content that directs your audience to a website where they can purchase a product or service, and you receive a commission or a fee for each sale or action that results from your link. For example, if you post a tweet with a link to an online bookstore where your followers can buy a book that you recommend, and you receive a percentage of the sales, you need to disclose that this is an affiliate or referral link.

Product or service reviews: This is when you provide your opinion or evaluation of a product or service that you have used or experienced, and you have a relationship or connection with the entity that provides or sells the product or service. For example, if you post a tweet with a video review of a smartphone that you received for free from the manufacturer, you need to disclose that this is a product or service review.

Brand or partner affiliations: This is when you have an ongoing or long-term relationship or connection with a brand, partner, or entity that you mention or promote in your content, and you receive benefits or incentives from them. For example, if you are an ambassador or a spokesperson for a sports brand, and you post tweets that feature or endorse their products, you need to disclose that this is a brand or partner affiliation.

How to disclose your partnerships, endorsements, and affiliations?

There are different ways to disclose your partnerships, endorsements, and affiliations on Twitter, but the general principles are the same.
Here are some tips and best practices on how to disclose your relationships:

Follow the Twitter advertising policies and the FTC guidelines on endorsements: Before you create or share any content that involves a partnership, endorsement, or affiliation, you should familiarize yourself with the Twitter advertising policies **https://business.twitter.com/en/help/ads-policies/introduction-**

to-twitter-ads/twitter-ads-policies.html and the FTC guidelines on endorsements **https://www.ftc.gov/tips-advice/business-center/guidance/ftcs-endorsement-guides-what-people-are-asking.** These policies and guidelines provide detailed information and examples on what types of disclosures are required and how to make them. You should also check the laws and regulations that apply to your content in your country or region, as they may differ from the Twitter and FTC standards.

Use clear and conspicuous language and symbols: When you disclose your relationships, you should use clear and conspicuous language and symbols that your audience can easily understand and notice. You should avoid using vague, ambiguous, or misleading terms or expressions, such as **thanks**, **partner**, or **collab**. You should also avoid using symbols or abbreviations that are not widely recognized or understood, such as **#, spon**, or **ad**. Instead, you should use explicit and unambiguous terms or expressions, such as **paid, sponsored, ad**, or **affiliate**. You should also use symbols or abbreviations that are commonly used and accepted, such as **$, AD**, or **SPON**.

Place the disclosure at the beginning or within the content: When you disclose your relationships, you should place the disclosure at the beginning or within the content, so that your audience can see it before they engage with your content. You should avoid placing the disclosure at the end or outside the content, such as in a separate tweet, a reply, or a bio. This is because your audience may not see or notice the disclosure if they only see or interact with your main content. For example, if you post a tweet with a video that is paid or sponsored by a brand, you should include the disclosure in the tweet text or in the video itself, rather than in a follow-up tweet or a comment.

Be honest and accurate about your relationship and experience: When you disclose your relationships, you should be honest and accurate about the nature and extent of your relationship with the entities or products that you mention or promote in your content. You should not exaggerate, embellish, or fabricate your relationship or connection, or imply that you have a relationship or connection that you do not have. You should also be honest and accurate about your experience or opinion of the products or services that you feature or endorse in your content. You should not make false, misleading, or unsubstantiated claims or statements, or omit or conceal any material facts or information that may affect your audience's decision or judgment.

Protecting your reputation and credibility by disclosing your partnerships, endorsements, and affiliations is an essential part of creating and sharing content on Twitter. By following the tips and best practices outlined above, you can ensure that you are honest, transparent, and compliant with your audience, the platform, and the law. You can also avoid negative consequences for your reputation and credibility, and maintain a positive and respectful relationship with your followers, partners, and peers.

Handle Negative Feedback, Criticism, and Complaints.

As a Twitter user, you may encounter negative feedback, criticism, and complaints from other users who disagree with you, are dissatisfied with your content, or have some issues with your products or services. These can be challenging and unpleasant situations, but they are also opportunities to learn, improve, and build trust and loyalty with your audience. Therefore, it is important to handle negative feedback, criticism, and complaints professionally and respectfully.

Types of Negative Feedback, Criticism, and Complaints:

Negative feedback, criticism, and complaints can come in various forms and degrees of severity. Some of the common types that you may face are:

Disagreement or dissatisfaction with your content or opinion: This is when someone expresses a different point of view or preference from yours or is unhappy with what you post or share. For example, someone may comment on your tweet that they disagree with your political stance, or that they did not like your latest video or blog post.

Accusation or suspicion of dishonesty or bias: This is when someone questions your credibility, integrity, or motives, or accuses you of being dishonest, biased, or misleading. For example, someone may reply to your tweet that you are lying about a fact, or that you are promoting a product or service for personal gain or favor.

Request or demand for refund or compensation: This is when someone asks or demands that you give them back their money or provide them with some form of compensation for a product or service that they bought from you or through your recommendation. For example, someone may message you that they want a refund for a course or ebook that they purchased from your website, or that they want you to pay for the damages caused by a product that you endorsed or sponsored.

Personal attack or insult: This is when someone attacks or insults you personally, rather than your content, product, or service. For example, someone may tweet at you that you are stupid, ugly, or worthless, or that they hate you or wish you harm.

Tips and Best Practices on How to Handle Negative Feedback, Criticism, and Complaints:

Negative feedback, criticism, and complaints can be difficult to deal with, especially if they are harsh, unfair, or abusive. However, there are some tips and best practices that can help you handle them effectively and gracefully. Here are some of them:

Monitor and respond to your mentions and messages: It is important to keep track of what people are saying about you and your content, product, or service, and to respond to them promptly and politely. This shows that you care about your audience and their feedback and that you are willing to engage with them and address their concerns. You can use tools like Twitter notifications, mentions, and direct messages to monitor and respond to your feedback.

Acknowledge and apologize for any mistakes or issues: If you have made a mistake or caused an issue, you should acknowledge it and apologize for it sincerely and humbly. This shows that you are honest, accountable, and respectful and that you value your reputation and relationship with your audience. You should also explain what caused the mistake or issue, and what you are doing or have done to fix it or prevent it from happening again.

Provide explanation or clarification if needed: If there is a misunderstanding or confusion, you should provide an explanation or clarification to clear it up. This shows that you are transparent, informative, and helpful and that you want to communicate clearly and accurately with your audience. You should also provide evidence or sources to back up your claims or arguments, if applicable.

Offer a solution or resolution if possible: If there is a problem or complaint, you should offer a solution or resolution to solve it or satisfy it. This shows that you are solution-oriented, customer-focused, and generous and that you want to provide value and quality to your audience. You should also follow up with your audience to make sure that they are happy with the solution or resolution, and to thank them for their feedback and support.

Ignore or block trolls or abusive users: If there is a troll or abusive user who is harassing, bullying, or spamming you or your audience, you should ignore or block them. This shows that you are confident, assertive, and protective, and that you do not tolerate or engage with negativity or toxicity. You should also report them to Twitter if they violate the Twitter rules or policies.

Recover from Setbacks and Failures.

Twitter is a dynamic and competitive platform, where users constantly strive to grow their audience, influence, and income. However, not everything always goes according to plan, and sometimes users may face setbacks and failures that can affect their performance and reputation. In this subchapter, we will explain why it is important to recover from setbacks and failures, and how to do it effectively and efficiently.

Why is it important to recover from setbacks and failures?

Setbacks and failures are inevitable in any endeavor, especially in a fast-paced and constantly changing environment like Twitter. They can be caused by various factors, such as:

Changes in the market trends, user preferences, or algorithms.
Mistakes, errors, or oversights in your content, strategy, or execution.
Unforeseen events, circumstances, or challenges that are beyond your control.
Competition, criticism, or opposition from other users or stakeholders.

Setbacks and failures can have negative impacts on your Twitter account, such as:

Loss of followers or engagement
Drop in income or revenue
Negative feedback or reviews
Technical or operational issues
Legal or ethical problems

These impacts can damage your confidence, motivation, and reputation, and make you feel discouraged, frustrated, or hopeless. However, setbacks and failures are not the end of the world, and they can also be valuable opportunities for learning, improvement, and growth. By recovering from setbacks and failures, you can:

Identify and correct your weaknesses, gaps, or flaws
Enhance your skills, knowledge, or abilities
Adapt to the changing needs, demands, or expectations of your audience and the platform
Innovate and create new or better solutions, products, or services
Strengthen your resilience, perseverance, and determination
Increase your credibility, trustworthiness, and loyalty among your followers and customers

Therefore, recovering from setbacks and failures is crucial for your success and sustainability on Twitter, as it can help you overcome challenges, achieve your goals, and fulfill your potential.

How to recover from setbacks and failures?

Recovering from setbacks and failures is not easy, but it is possible and rewarding. Here are some tips and best practices that can help you recover from setbacks and failures on Twitter:

Analyze and evaluate the causes and effects of the setback or failure: The first step to recovery from a setback or failure is to understand what went wrong, why it went wrong, and how it affected you and your account. This can help you avoid repeating the same mistakes, and learn from your experience. To analyze and evaluate the causes and effects of the setback or failure, you can:

Review your data, metrics, or analytics to measure your performance and identify the areas that need improvement.

Conduct a SWOT analysis (Strengths, Weaknesses, Opportunities, Threats) to assess your internal and external factors that influenced the outcome.

Use the 5 Whys technique to dig deeper into the root causes of the problem and find the underlying reasons behind it.

Use the SMART framework (Specific, Measurable, Achievable, Relevant, Time-bound) to set realistic and actionable goals for your recovery and improvement.

Identify and implement the necessary changes or improvements: The second step to recover from a setback or failure is to take action and make the changes or improvements that can help you solve the problem and prevent it from happening again. This can help you improve your performance and reputation, and achieve your goals. To identify and implement the necessary changes or improvements, you can:

Brainstorm and research possible solutions, alternatives, or options that can address the issue and meet your needs and objectives.

Test and evaluate the effectiveness, feasibility, and suitability of the solutions, alternatives, or options before implementing them.

Implement the chosen solution, alternative, or option in a timely and efficient manner, and monitor its results and impacts

Review and refine the solution, alternative, or option as needed, based on the feedback and outcomes

Seek feedback or advice from your peers or mentors: The third step to recover from a setback or failure is to seek feedback or advice from your peers or mentors who can offer you support, guidance, or insight. This can help you gain new perspectives, ideas, or suggestions, and learn from others' experiences and expertise. To seek feedback or advice from your peers or mentors, you can:

Join or create a network, community, or group of Twitter users who share your niche, interests, or goals, and exchange information, opinions, or tips with them.

Follow or contact Twitter users who are successful, influential, or reputable in your field, and ask them for feedback, advice, or recommendations.

Participate in online or offline events, workshops, or courses related to your topic, industry, or profession, and network with other participants, speakers, or instructors.

Hire or consult a professional, expert, or coach who can provide you with personalized, tailored, or specialized feedback, advice, or assistance.

Celebrate your achievements and progress: The fourth step to recover from a setback or failure is to celebrate your achievements and progress, no matter how big or small they are. This can help you boost your morale, confidence, and motivation, and appreciate your efforts and results. To celebrate your achievements and progress, you can:

Acknowledge and reward yourself for reaching a milestone, completing a task, or overcoming a challenge.

Share your success stories, lessons learned, or best practices with your followers, customers, or partners, and thank them for their support, trust, or collaboration.

Showcase your portfolio, testimonials, or case studies to demonstrate your value, quality, or impact.

Set new or higher goals, standards, or expectations for yourself, and challenge yourself to achieve them.

Stay positive and motivated: The fifth and final step to recover from a setback or failure is to stay positive and motivated, and not let the negative emotions or thoughts overwhelm you or stop you from trying again. This can help you cope with stress, anxiety, or fear, and maintain your enthusiasm, passion, and vision. To stay positive and motivated, you can:

Adopt a growth mindset, which believes that you can learn, grow, and improve from any situation and that challenges are opportunities, not threats.

Practice gratitude, optimism, or affirmations, which can help you focus on the positive aspects, outcomes, or possibilities of your situation, and enhance your mood, attitude, or outlook

Seek inspiration, motivation, or encouragement from sources that can uplift, energize, or empower you, such as books, podcasts, videos, quotes, or stories

Take care of your physical, mental, and emotional health and well-being, by doing activities that can relax, rejuvenate, or refresh you, such as exercise, meditation, hobbies, or fun.

In this chapter, we have discussed some of the common mistakes that can hinder your success in earning income from Twitter. We have also provided some tips and strategies on how to avoid or overcome these mistakes and achieve your goals.

One of the most important aspects of using Twitter as an income source is to understand and comply with the rules and policies that govern the platform and the income opportunities. These rules and policies are designed to protect the integrity, safety, and quality of the Twitter community and the user experience. Violating them can result in penalties, suspensions, or bans from the platform or the income programs. Therefore, you should always read and follow the guidelines and terms of service of Twitter and its partners, and keep yourself updated on any changes or updates.

Another common mistake that can affect your income potential is to overdo your promotional content and spam your followers with too many ads, links, or offers. This can annoy or alienate your followers and make them lose interest or trust in you. To avoid this, you should balance your promotional and non-promotional content and provide value and engagement to your followers. You should also use the appropriate tools and methods to promote your products, services, or affiliates, such as hashtags, mentions, retweets, direct messages, or Twitter cards.

A related mistake that can damage your reputation and credibility is to fail to disclose your partnerships, endorsements, or affiliations with the brands, products, or services that you promote or recommend on Twitter. This can be seen as deceptive or unethical by your followers and the regulators and can expose you to legal risks or fines. To avoid this, you should always be transparent and honest about your relationships with the entities that you work with or benefit from, and use the proper disclosure methods, such as hashtags, labels, or disclaimers.

Another common mistake that can affect your income and growth is to handle negative feedback, criticism, or complaints in a wrong or unprofessional way. This can harm your image and reputation and cause you to lose followers or customers. To avoid this, you should always respond to negative feedback respectfully and constructively, and try to resolve the issues or concerns that your followers or customers may have. You should also avoid engaging in arguments, insults, or attacks with your critics, and block or report any abusive or harassing behavior.

Finally, another common mistake that can hinder your progress and success is to give up or lose motivation when you face setbacks or failures in your income endeavors. This can prevent you from learning from your mistakes and improving your skills and strategies. To avoid this, you should always have a positive and resilient attitude and treat your setbacks or failures as opportunities to learn and grow. You should also seek feedback, advice, or support from your peers, mentors, or experts, and keep yourself informed and inspired by the latest trends, changes, and developments in the Twitter income landscape.

By avoiding these common mistakes, you can increase your chances of earning income from Twitter and achieving your financial goals.

Chapter Seven

Innovative Tips for Success.

In the previous chapters, we have covered the basics of how to generate income from Twitter, such as choosing your niche, creating your profile, building your audience, and monetizing your content. However, if you want to take your Twitter income to the next level, you need to be more innovative and creative in your approach. We will share some tips and tricks that can help you achieve greater success and satisfaction from your Twitter income activities. Specifically, we will discuss the following topics:

Experimenting and testing new features, formats, and strategies. Twitter is constantly evolving and introducing new ways for users to create and consume content. You can use these opportunities to experiment and test different features, formats, and strategies to see what works best for your niche, audience, and goals. For example, you can try using Twitter Spaces, Fleets, Super Follows, Tip Jar, or Twitter Blue to enhance your engagement, reach, and income.

Leveraging tools and resources that can help you automate, streamline, and enhance your Twitter income activities. Managing your Twitter income can be time-consuming and challenging, especially if you have multiple accounts, platforms, or income streams. Fortunately, many tools and resources can help you automate, streamline, and enhance your Twitter income activities, such as scheduling tools, analytics tools, content creation tools, and learning resources. We will introduce some of the best tools and resources that you can use to save time, optimize your performance, and increase your income.

Collaborating and networking with other Twitter users, influencers, and experts. Twitter is not only a platform for creating and sharing content, but also a platform for connecting and interacting with other people. You can use Twitter to collaborate and network with other Twitter users, influencers, and experts in your niche or industry, to learn, exchange, and support each other. For example, you can join or create Twitter chats, lists, groups, or communities, participate in or host Twitter events, webinars, or podcasts, or reach out to or partner with other Twitter users, influencers, or experts for cross-promotion, guest posting, or sponsorship opportunities.

Diversifying and expanding your income streams and sources. Relying on a single or limited income stream or source can be risky and limiting, as it can be affected by various factors, such as algorithm changes, policy updates, market trends, or audience preferences. To reduce your risks and increase your earning potential, you should diversify and expand your income streams and sources, by exploring and experimenting with different ways to monetize your Twitter presence, content, skills, or knowledge. For example, you can create and sell your products or services, join or create your own affiliate or referral programs, or offer coaching, consulting, or mentoring services.

Setting and tracking your goals and milestones and celebrating your achievements. Having clear and realistic goals and milestones can help you stay focused, motivated, and accountable for your Twitter income activities. You should set and track your goals and milestones, using SMART criteria (Specific, Measurable, Achievable, Relevant, and Time-bound), and using tools and methods that suit your preferences and needs. You should also celebrate your achievements, no matter how big or small, by rewarding yourself, sharing your success stories, or expressing your gratitude to your supporters.

Continuously learning and improving your skills and knowledge in Twitter income generation. Twitter income generation is a dynamic and competitive field, that requires constant learning and improvement. You should always be curious and eager to learn new things and improve your skills and knowledge in Twitter income generation, by reading, watching, listening, or attending relevant and credible sources of information, such as blogs, books, videos, podcasts, courses, or events. You should also seek and apply feedback, from your audience, peers, mentors, or experts, to identify and address your strengths and weaknesses, and to grow and improve your Twitter income activities.

By following these tips and tricks, you will be able to innovate and excel in your Twitter income activities and enjoy the benefits and rewards of your hard work and creativity. In the next section, we will dive deeper into each of these topics, and provide you with more examples, insights, and resources to help you implement them in your own Twitter income journey.

Experimenting and testing new features, formats, and strategies to optimize your Twitter income.

Twitter is a dynamic and evolving platform that offers a variety of ways to monetize your content and audience. However, not every method or approach will work for everyone. That's why it's important to experiment and test different aspects of your Twitter income activities to find out what works best for you and your followers.

Why experiment and test?

Experimenting and testing are essential for optimizing your Twitter income performance because they allow you to:

Discover new opportunities and trends that you can leverage to grow your audience and income.
Identify and eliminate the factors that are holding you back or costing you money.
Learn from your own experience and data, rather than relying on assumptions or generalizations.
Adapt to the changing preferences and behaviors of your followers and potential customers.
Improve your content quality and value proposition
Increase your engagement and conversion rates
Enhance your brand image and reputation

How to experiment and test?

There are many ways to experiment and test different aspects of your Twitter income activities, but here are some general steps that you can follow:

Define your goal and hypothesis: What do you want to achieve and what do you think will help you achieve it?

Choose your variable and control: What are you going to change and what are you going to keep constant?

Design your experiment and test: How are you going to implement and measure your change?

Run your experiment and test: How long are you going to run your experiment and test for and how are you going to collect and record your data?

Analyze your results and draw conclusions: What did you learn from your experiment and test and what does it mean for your goal and hypothesis?

Apply your findings and recommendations: How are you going to use your insights and feedback to improve your Twitter income performance?

What to experiment and test?

There are many aspects of your Twitter income activities that you can experiment and test, such as:

New features and formats: Twitter is constantly introducing new features and formats that you can use to create and monetize your content, such as Twitter Spaces, Fleets, Super Follows, Tip Jar, Ticketed Spaces, etc. You can experiment and test these features and formats to see how they affect your audience size, engagement, and income. For example, you can try hosting a live audio chat with your followers using Twitter Spaces and see how many people join, how long they stay, and how much they tip you.

Or you can try creating short-lived posts using Fleets and see how they increase your visibility and reach.

Different types of content: Twitter allows you to create and share different types of content, such as images, videos, polls, quizzes, threads, etc. You can experiment and test these types of content to see how they resonate with your followers and potential customers. For example, you can try posting a video tutorial of your product or service and see how it boosts your sales. Or you can try posting a poll or a quiz to get feedback from your followers and see how it improves your relationship with them.

Different posting times, frequencies, lengths, hashtags, etc.: Twitter has its algorithms and rules that determine how your content is distributed and displayed to your followers and potential customers. You can experiment and test these factors to see how they influence your exposure and performance. For example, you can try posting at different times of the day or week and see how it affects your impressions and clicks. Or you can try posting more or less frequently and see how it affects your retention and loyalty. Or you can try posting longer or shorter tweets and see how it affects your readability and engagement. Or you can try using different hashtags and see how it affects your discoverability and relevance.

How to measure and analyze.

To measure and analyze the results of your experiments and tests, you need to use various tools and metrics that can help you track and evaluate your Twitter income performance. Some of the tools and metrics that you can use are:

Twitter Analytics: Twitter provides its analytics dashboard that you can access from your profile or settings. It shows you various statistics and insights about your account, such as your tweet activity, audience demographics, top tweets, impressions, engagements, etc. You can use this tool to monitor and compare your performance before and after your experiments and tests.

Google Analytics: Google Analytics is a web analytics service that you can use to measure and analyze your website traffic and conversions. If you have a website or a landing page that you link to from your Twitter account, you can use this tool to track and evaluate how your Twitter activity drives traffic and sales to your website or landing page. You can also use this tool to set up goals and experiments to test different versions of your website or landing page and see which one performs better.

Bitly: Bitly is a link management platform that you can use to shorten and customize your links. If you use links in your tweets, you can use this tool to create and track your links and see how they perform in terms of clicks, referrals, conversions, etc. You can also use this tool to create and test different variations of your links and see which one generates more clicks and conversions.

Social Blade: Social Blade is a social media analytics tool that you can use to measure and analyze your social media presence and growth. You can use this tool to compare your Twitter account with other Twitter accounts in terms of followers, following, tweets, etc. You can also use this tool to see how your Twitter account ranks among other Twitter accounts in your niche or category.

How to apply and improve.

To apply and improve your Twitter income performance based on the results of your experiments and tests, you need to:

Validate or invalidate your hypothesis: Based on your analysis and conclusions, you need to determine whether your hypothesis was correct or incorrect. If your hypothesis was correct, you can confirm that your change was effective and beneficial. If your hypothesis was incorrect, you can reject that your change was ineffective or detrimental.

Implement or discard your change: Based on your validation or invalidation, you need to decide whether to implement or discard your change. If your change is effective and beneficial, you can implement it permanently or scale it up. If your change was ineffective or detrimental, you can discard it or scale it down.

Repeat or refine your experiment and test: Based on your implementation or discarding, you need to decide whether to repeat or refine your experiment and test. If your change was effective and beneficial, you can repeat your experiment and test to verify and consolidate your results. If your change was ineffective or detrimental, you can refine your experiment and test to improve and optimize your results.

Leveraging tools and resources that can help you automate, streamline, and enhance your Twitter income activities.

Twitter is a powerful platform for generating income from your online presence, whether you are a creator, influencer, entrepreneur, or educator. However, managing your Twitter income activities can be time-consuming, complex, and challenging. That's why it is important to leverage the tools and resources that can help you automate, streamline, and enhance your Twitter income activities.

Advantages and challenges of using tools and resources:

Using tools and resources to support your Twitter income activities can offer many advantages, such as:

Saving time and energy by automating repetitive tasks, such as content creation, curation, scheduling, audience engagement, growth, retention, monetization, payment, and donation.

Improving your productivity and efficiency by streamlining your workflow and processes, such as managing multiple accounts, tracking your performance and analytics, and optimizing your strategy and tactics.

Boosting your creativity and quality by enhancing your content and offers, such as designing eye-catching graphics, videos, and podcasts, creating engaging and valuable tweets and threads, and delivering exclusive and premium content and services.

However, using tools and resources also comes with some challenges, such as:

Finding the right tools and resources that suit your needs, goals, and budget, among the plethora of options available in the market.

Learning how to use the tools and resources effectively and efficiently, by understanding their features, functions, and limitations, and following their guidelines and best practices.

Balancing the use of tools and resources with your voice, personality, and authenticity, by avoiding over-reliance, misuse, or abuse of the tools and resources, and maintaining your human connection and interaction with your audience.

Examples and reviews of some of the best tools and resources:

There are many tools and resources available for Twitter income earners, depending on your niche, audience, and business model. Here are some examples and reviews of some of the best tools and resources in four categories:

Tools for content creation, curation, and scheduling: These tools help you create, curate, and schedule your content for Twitter, such as tweets, threads, graphics, videos, and podcasts.

Canva: Canva is a graphic design tool that allows you to create stunning visuals for your Twitter content, such as banners, logos, infographics, flyers, and more. You can use Canva's templates, icons, fonts, and images, or upload your own. You can also edit, resize, and download your designs in various formats. Canva has a free plan and a pro plan that offers more features and resources.

Canva is easy to use, versatile, and affordable, and it integrates with other tools such as Buffer and Hootsuite.

Buffer: Buffer is a social media management tool that allows you to schedule and publish your tweets and threads, as well as other social media posts, from one dashboard. You can also monitor and analyze your Twitter performance and engagement, and get insights and recommendations to improve your strategy. Buffer has a free plan and a pro plan that offers more features and accounts. Buffer is simple, user-friendly, and reliable, and it integrates with other tools such as Canva and TweetDeck.

Hootsuite: Hootsuite is another social media management tool that allows you to schedule and publish your tweets and threads, as well as other social media posts, from one dashboard. You can also monitor and analyze your Twitter performance and engagement, and get insights and recommendations to improve your strategy. Hootsuite has a free plan and a pro plan that offers more features and accounts. Hootsuite is more comprehensive, advanced, and customizable than Buffer, but it can also be more complicated and expensive.

Tools for audience engagement, growth, and retention: These tools help you engage, grow, and retain your audience on Twitter, such as followers, fans, and customers.
TweetDeck: TweetDeck is a Twitter dashboard that allows you to manage multiple Twitter accounts, monitor and interact with your Twitter activity, such as mentions, messages, notifications, and trends, and create and schedule your tweets and threads. TweetDeck is free and easy to use, and it integrates with other tools such as Buffer and Sprout Social.

Sprout Social: Sprout Social is a social media management and analytics tool that allows you to manage multiple Twitter accounts, monitor and interact with your Twitter activity, such as mentions, messages, notifications, and trends, and create and schedule your tweets and threads. You can also measure and optimize your Twitter performance and engagement, and get insights and recommendations to improve your strategy. Sprout Social has a free trial and a pro plan that offers more features and accounts. Sprout Social is more robust, sophisticated, and professional than TweetDeck, but it can also be more costly and complex.

Crowdfire: Crowdfire is a social media marketing and growth tool that allows you to manage multiple Twitter accounts, monitor and interact with your Twitter activity, such as mentions, messages, notifications, and trends, and create and schedule your tweets and threads. You can also discover and curate relevant content for your Twitter audience, and grow and retain your Twitter followers, fans, and customers. Crowdfire has a free plan and a pro plan that offers more features and accounts. Crowdfire is more focused, targeted, and effective than TweetDeck and Sprout Social, but it can also be more restrictive and intrusive.

Tools for monetization, payment, and donation: These tools help you monetize, receive, and send money on Twitter, such as tips, donations, subscriptions, and sales.
Patreon: Patreon is a platform that allows you to create and offer exclusive and premium content and services to your Twitter audience, such as behind-the-scenes, early access, bonus episodes, Q&A sessions, and more. You can also set up different tiers and rewards for your patrons, and receive recurring monthly payments from them. Patreon has a free plan and a pro plan that offers more features and resources. Patreon is easy to use, flexible, and popular, and it integrates with other tools such as PayPal and Stripe.

PayPal: PayPal is a payment service that allows you to receive and send money on Twitter, such as tips, donations, subscriptions, and sales. You can also create and send invoices, receipts, and refunds, and manage your transactions and accounts. PayPal has a free plan and a pro plan that offers more features and services. PayPal is secure, convenient, and widely accepted, and it integrates with other tools such as Patreon and Stripe.

Stripe: Stripe is another payment service that allows you to receive and send money on Twitter, such as tips, donations, subscriptions, and sales. You can also create and send invoices, receipts, and refunds, and manage your transactions and accounts. Stripe has a free plan and a pro plan that offers more features and services. Stripe is more modern, innovative, and customizable than PayPal, but it can also be more difficult and expensive.

Resources for learning, inspiration, and guidance: These resources help you learn, inspire, and guide you on your Twitter income journey, such as blogs, podcasts, courses, books, and more.

Blogs: Blogs are online articles that provide information, insights, and tips on various topics related to Twitter income, such as content creation, audience engagement, monetization, and more. Some of the best blogs for Twitter income earners are:

Twitter Business Blog **https://business.twitter.com/en/blog.html**: This is the official blog of Twitter for business, where you can find the latest news, updates, and best practices for using Twitter to grow your brand, reach your audience, and drive your results.

Buffer Blog **https://buffer.com/resources/**: This is the blog of Buffer, where you can find practical and actionable advice on how to use social media to build your online presence, engage your audience, and grow your business.

Hootsuite Blog **https://blog.hootsuite.com/**: This is the blog of Hootsuite, where you can find expert and in-depth guidance on how to use social media to achieve your goals, overcome your challenges, and stay ahead of the trends.

Podcasts: Podcasts are audio shows that provide information, insights, and tips on various topics related to Twitter income, such as content creation, audience engagement, monetization, and more. Some of the best podcasts for Twitter income earners are:

The Twitter Smarter Podcast **https://madalynsklar.com/twittersmarter-podcast/**: This is a podcast hosted by Madalyn Sklar, a Twitter marketing expert, where you can learn how to use Twitter to get more followers, more engagement, and more results.

The Social Media Marketing Podcast **https://www.socialmediaexaminer.com/shows/**: This is a podcast hosted by Michael Stelzner, the founder of Social Media Examiner, where you can discover how successful businesses use social media to market their products and services, and how you can apply their strategies to your own business.

The Smart Passive Income Podcast **https://www.smartpassiveincome.com/podcasts/**: This is a podcast hosted by Pat Flynn, a successful online entrepreneur, where you can learn how to create and grow your online business, generate passive income, and achieve your financial and lifestyle goals.

Courses: Courses are online or offline programs that provide information, insights, and tips on various topics related to Twitter income, such as content creation, audience engagement, monetization, and more. Some of the best courses for Twitter income earners are:

Twitter Flight School **https://twitterflightschool.com/**: This is an online course offered by Twitter, where you can learn how to use Twitter to market your brand, reach your audience, and drive your results. You can choose from different modules and tracks, such as Twitter Video, Twitter Ads, and Twitter Analytics, and get certified by Twitter upon completion.

Social Media Marketing Mastery **https://www.udemy.com/course/social-media-marketing-mastery/**: This is an online course offered by Udemy, where you can learn how to use social media to grow your online presence, engage your audience, and grow your business. You can learn from various instructors and experts, such as Ryan Hildreth, Adam Reed, and Phil Ebiner, and get access to over 10 hours of video content and 75 lectures.

Books: Books are printed or digital publications that provide information, insights, and tips on various topics related to Twitter income, such as content creation, audience engagement, monetization, and more. Some of the best books for Twitter income earners are:

Twitter Marketing for Dummies **https://www.amazon.com/Twitter-Marketing-Dummies-Kyle-Lacy/dp/0470930578**: This is a book by Kyle Lacy, a social media expert, where you can learn how to use Twitter to market your brand, reach your audience, and drive your results. You can learn the basics of Twitter, such as setting up your profile, tweeting, and following, as well as advanced strategies, such as building your network, engaging your followers, and measuring your impact.

The Tao of Twitter **https://www.amazon.com/Tao-Twitter-Changing-Business-Connections/dp/0071841156**: This is a book by Mark Schaefer, a marketing consultant, and professor, where you can learn how to use Twitter to create meaningful and authentic connections and grow your online influence and authority. You can learn the principles and practices of Twitter, such as finding your target audience, creating valuable content, and building relationships, as well as case studies and examples of successful Twitter users.

Twitter Power 3.0 **https://www.amazon.com/Twitter-Power-3-0-Everything-Generate/dp/1119021812**: This is a book by Joel Comm, a social media entrepreneur, and speaker, where you can learn how to use Twitter to generate income from your online presence and leverage the latest features and trends of Twitter. You can learn the tips and tricks of Twitter, such as optimizing your profile, using hashtags, and live-streaming, as well as monetization methods, such as advertising, sponsoring, and selling.

Tips and best practices for choosing and using the right tools and resources.

Choosing and using the right tools and resources for your Twitter income activities can be overwhelming and confusing, given the variety and complexity of the options available. Here are some tips and best practices to help you make the best decisions and get the most out of the tools and resources:

Define your goals and needs: Before you choose and use any tool or resource, you need to have a clear idea of what you want to achieve and what you need to do. For example, do you want to increase your followers, engagement, or revenue? Do you need to create, curate, or schedule your content? Do you need to monitor, analyze, or optimize your performance? Do you need to learn, inspire, or guide yourself or others?

Do your research and comparison: Once you have defined your goals and needs, you need to do your research and comparison of the different tools and resources that can help you meet them. For example, you can read reviews, ratings, testimonials, and feedback from other users, experts, and influencers. You can also compare the features, functions, benefits, and costs of the different tools and resources, and see which ones suit your preferences, expectations, and budget.

Try before you buy: After you have done your research and comparison, you need to try before you buy any tool or resource that you are interested in. For example, you can sign up for free trials, plans, or accounts, and test the tools and resources for yourself. You can also look for demos, tutorials, or guides that can help you learn how to use the tools and resources effectively and efficiently.

Evaluate and adjust: Finally, after you have tried and bought any tool or resource that you are satisfied with, you need to evaluate and adjust your use of them regularly. For example, you can measure and track your results and outcomes, and see if they match your goals and needs. You can also look for feedback, support, or updates that can help you improve your use of the tools and resources. You can also explore new or alternative tools and resources that can offer you more value or convenience.

Collaborating and networking with other Twitter users, influencers, and experts to learn, exchange, and support each other.

One of the best ways to grow your Twitter income is to collaborate and network with other Twitter users, influencers, and experts in your niche or industry. By doing so, you can:

Gain knowledge from their lessons, perspectives, and effective methods.
Exchange ideas, resources, and opportunities.
Support each other's goals, challenges, and achievements.

Collaborating and networking with other Twitter users, influencers, and experts can help you:

Increase your reach and visibility by exposing your content and brand to new and relevant audiences.

Boost your credibility and authority. by associating yourself with reputable and influential figures in your field.

Enhance your creativity and innovation by getting inspired and challenged by different perspectives and approaches.

Expand your income streams and opportunities by discovering and creating new ways to monetize your Twitter presence and skills.

Examples and stories of successful collaborations and networks formed by other Twitter income earners:

There are many examples and stories of how other Twitter income earners have benefited from collaborating and networking with other Twitter users, influencers, and experts. Here are some of them:

Co-creating and cross-promoting content with other Twitter users, influencers, and experts:

Co-creating and cross-promoting content with other Twitter users, influencers, and experts can help you create more value and variety for your audience, as well as increase your exposure and engagement.

For example, James Clear **https://twitter.com/JamesClear**, a bestselling author and Twitter income earner, often co-creates and cross-promotes content with other authors, such as Adam Grant **https://twitter.com/AdamMGrant**, Ryan Holiday **https://twitter.com/RyanHoliday**, and Mark Manson **https://twitter.com/IAmMarkManson**. They share each other's books, articles, podcasts, and newsletters, as well as engage in conversations and debates on Twitter. This way, they can reach and attract more readers, listeners, and subscribers, as well as showcase their expertise and thought leadership.

Participating and hosting Twitter chats, Spaces, events, etc. with other Twitter users, influencers, and experts:

Participating and hosting Twitter chats, Spaces, events, etc. with other Twitter users, influencers, and experts can help you build relationships, share knowledge, and generate buzz around your topic or niche.

For example, Pat Flynn **https://twitter.com/PatFlynn**, a successful online entrepreneur and Twitter income earner, regularly participates and hosts Twitter chats, Spaces, events, etc. with other online entrepreneurs, such as Amy Porterfield **https://twitter.com/AmyPorterfield**, John Lee Dumas **https://twitter.com/johnleedumas**, and Chris Ducker **https://twitter.com/ChrisDucker.** They discuss various aspects of online business, such as marketing, podcasting, blogging, etc., and answer questions from their followers. This way, they can provide value and education to their audience, as well as promote their products and services.

Joining and creating online communities, groups, forums, etc. with other Twitter users, influencers, and experts:

Joining and creating online communities, groups, forums, etc. with other Twitter users, influencers, and experts can help you connect with like-minded people, exchange feedback and support, and discover new opportunities and collaborations.

For example, Ali Abdaal **https://twitter.com/AliAbdaal**, a popular YouTube creator and Twitter income earner, has created an online community called The Part-Time YouTuber Academy **https://academy.aliabdaal.com/**, where he teaches and mentors aspiring and existing YouTube creators. He also invites other YouTube creators, such as Thomas Frank **https://twitter.com/tomfrankly**, Matt D'Avella **https://twitter.com/mattdavella**, and Marques Brownlee **https://twitter.com/MKBHD**, to join and share their tips and tricks. This way, he can create a loyal and engaged fan base, as well as generate income from his courses and memberships.

Seeking and offering mentorship, advice, feedback, etc. with other Twitter users, influencers, and experts:

Seeking and offering mentorship, advice, feedback, etc. with other Twitter users, influencers, and experts can help you improve your skills, overcome your challenges, and achieve your goals.

For example, Tim Ferriss **https://twitter.com/tferriss**, a renowned author and Twitter income earner, often seeks and offers mentorship, advice, feedback, etc. with other Twitter users, influencers, and experts, such as Naval Ravikant **https://twitter.com/naval**, Kevin Rose **https://twitter.com/kevinrose**, and Jack Dorsey. He asks them questions, interviews them, features them on his podcast and newsletter, and learns from their wisdom and experience. This way, he can grow his personal and professional development, as well as share valuable insights and stories with his audience.

Tips and strategies for finding and connecting with the right Twitter users, influencers, and experts for your Twitter income objectives and interests:

Finding and connecting with the right Twitter users, influencers, and experts for your Twitter income objectives and interests can be challenging, but not impossible. Here are some suggestions and methods to assist you:

Identify your niche and target audience: Before you start collaborating and networking with other Twitter users, influencers, and experts, you need to know who you are, what you do, and who you serve. This will help you narrow down your focus and find the most relevant and compatible people to connect with. Research and follow the top Twitter users, influencers, and experts in your niche or industry. Once you have identified your niche and target audience, you need to find out who are the top Twitter users, influencers, and experts in your field. You can use tools like Followerwonk **https://followerwonk.com/**, BuzzSumo **https://buzzsumo.com/**, or Twitter Lists **https://help.twitter.com/en/using-twitter/twitter-lists** to search and filter them by keywords, topics, location, followers, engagement, etc. You can then follow them, read their tweets, and learn from their content and style.

Engage with them authentically and respectfully: After you have followed the top Twitter users, influencers, and experts in your niche or industry, you need to engage with them authentically and respectfully. You can do this by liking, retweeting, commenting, replying, mentioning, or quoting their tweets, as well as joining their Twitter chats, Spaces, events, etc. You can also ask them questions, compliment them, thank them, or share your opinions and insights. However, you should avoid spamming, trolling, or being rude or pushy. You should aim to add value and build rapport, not annoy or offend them.

Reach out to them personally and professionally: Once you have engaged with the top Twitter users, influencers, and experts in your niche or industry, you can reach out to them personally and professionally. You can do this by sending them a direct message, an email, or a tweet, and expressing your interest in collaborating or networking with them. You can also invite them to your Twitter chats, Spaces, events, etc. or ask them to join or create online communities, groups, forums, etc. with you. However, you should be clear, concise, and courteous in your communication, and explain why you want to connect with them, what value you can offer them, and what you expect from them. You should also respect their time and availability, and follow up with them politely and patiently.

Diversifying and expanding your income streams and sources to increase your earning potential and reduce your risks.

As a Twitter income earner, you may be wondering how to make more money from your online presence and influence. You may also be concerned about the stability and security of your income, especially in times of uncertainty and change. How can you ensure that you have enough cash flow to support your lifestyle and goals, and that you are not dependent on a single source of income that may dry up or disappear?

The answer is to diversify and expand your income streams and sources. This means that you create and leverage multiple ways of generating income from your Twitter account and beyond, so that you have more options and opportunities to earn money, and that you reduce your risks of losing income due to factors beyond your control.

We will discuss the reasons and benefits of diversifying and expanding your income streams and sources as a Twitter income earner, provide examples and options of different income streams and sources that you can explore and pursue, and suggest some tips and steps for diversifying and expanding your income streams and sources.

Reasons and benefits of diversifying and expanding your income streams and sources as a Twitter income earner.

There are many reasons and benefits of diversifying and expanding your income streams and sources as a Twitter income earner, such as:

Increasing your earning potential: By creating and leveraging multiple income streams and sources, you can increase your total income and grow your wealth over time. You can also take advantage of different income models and strategies, such as recurring, passive, or scalable income, that can help you earn more money with less effort or time. You can also tap into different markets and niches, and reach more customers and clients, that may not be accessible or interested in your primary income stream or source.

Reducing your risks: By having multiple income streams and sources, you can reduce your risks of losing income due to factors beyond your control, such as algorithm changes, platform bans, policy updates, market shifts, competition, demand fluctuations, or other external events. You can also hedge against inflation, currency devaluation, or economic downturns, by having income streams and sources that are diversified across different industries, sectors, regions, or currencies. You can also protect yourself from personal or professional crises, such as illness, injury, burnout, or legal issues, by having income streams and sources that are not dependent on your presence, performance, or reputation.

Enhancing your creativity and value: By creating and leveraging multiple income streams and sources, you can enhance your creativity and value as a Twitter income earner. You can explore and experiment with different ideas, skills, passions, or interests, that can help you discover new ways of expressing yourself, serving your audience, or solving problems. You can also learn and develop new skills, knowledge, or experiences, that can help you improve your existing income streams and sources, or create new ones. You can also showcase and demonstrate your expertise, authority, or credibility, by creating and sharing valuable content, products, or services, that can attract and retain more followers, fans, or customers.

Examples and options of different income streams and sources that you can explore and pursue:

There are many examples and options of different income streams and sources that you can explore and pursue as a Twitter income earner, such as:

Selling your own products or services: You can create and sell your own products or services, such as e-books, courses, coaching, consulting, etc., that are related to your niche, topic, or brand, and that can provide value, benefit, or solution to your audience, followers, or customers. You can use your Twitter account to promote and market your products or services, and to drive traffic and conversions to your website, landing page, or sales funnel. You can also use your Twitter account to provide customer service, feedback, or support, and to build trust, loyalty, or referrals. Some examples of Twitter income earners who sell their own products or services are:

@JamesClear, who is the author of the best-selling book Atomic Habits, and who sells his book, courses, and newsletter on his website jamesclear.com

@MarieForleo, who is the founder of B-School, an online business and marketing training program, and who sells her program, book, and podcast on her website marieforleo.com

@GaryVee, who is the CEO of VaynerMedia, a digital marketing agency, and who sells his services, books, and merchandise on his website garyvaynerchuk.com

Promoting and earning commissions from other people's products or services: You can promote and earn commissions from other people's products or services, such as affiliate marketing, sponsored posts, etc., that are relevant, useful, or appealing to your niche, topic, or brand, and that can provide value, benefit, or solution to your audience, followers, or customers. You can use your Twitter account to recommend and endorse the products or services, and to share your affiliate links, coupon codes, or referral codes, that can track and reward your sales or leads. You can also use your Twitter account to provide honest reviews, testimonials, or case studies, and to answer questions, objections, or concerns. Some examples of Twitter income earners who promote and earn commissions from other people's products or services are:

@PatFlynn, who is the founder of Smart Passive Income, a website and podcast that teaches people how to make money online, and who earns commissions from promoting various tools, software, and resources on his website smartpassiveincome.com
@KimKardashian, who is a reality TV star and social media influencer, and who earns commissions from promoting various brands, products, and services on her Twitter account, such as SKIMS, KKW Beauty, and Uber Eats.
@TimFerriss, who is the author of The 4-Hour Workweek and other books, and who earns commissions from promoting various books, products, and services on his website **https://tim.blog/** and his podcast **The Tim Ferriss Show**.

Creating and monetizing your own content: You can create and monetize your own content, such as podcasts, videos, blogs, newsletters, etc., that are related to your niche, topic, or brand, and that can provide value, benefit, or solution to your audience, followers, or customers. You can use your Twitter account to share and distribute your content, and to drive traffic and engagement to your platform, channel, or medium. You can also use your Twitter account to interact and communicate with your audience, followers, or customers, and to solicit feedback, suggestions, or requests. You can monetize your content by using various methods, such as ads, sponsorships, donations, subscriptions, memberships, etc. Some examples of Twitter income earners who create and monetize their own content are:

@JoeRogan, who is the host of The Joe Rogan Experience, a popular podcast that features interviews with various guests, and who monetizes his podcast by using ads, sponsorships, and merchandise on his website joerogan.com.

@MrBeast, who is a YouTube star and philanthropist, and who monetizes his videos by using ads, sponsorships, and merchandise on his YouTube channel and his website shopmrbeast.com.

@CaseyNewton, who is a tech journalist and newsletter writer, and who monetizes his newsletter by using subscriptions and sponsorships on his platform **https://www.platformer.news/**.

Generating and receiving passive income: You can generate and receive passive income, such as ads, royalties, donations, etc., that are derived from your existing or previous work, assets, or investments, and that do not require your active involvement or participation. You can use your Twitter account to showcase and promote your work, assets, or investments, and to direct your audience, followers, or customers to your source of passive income. You can also use your Twitter account to provide updates, reports, or insights, and to thank or acknowledge your supporters, contributors, or partners. Some examples of Twitter income earners who generate and receive passive income are:

@jk_rowling, the author of the Harry Potter series and other books, receives royalties from her books, movies, games, and merchandise on her website.

@Passive_IncomeG is a blogger and podcaster who shares tips and strategies on how to create passive income streams from various sources, such as affiliate marketing, e-commerce, and online courses.

@taylorswift13, is a singer-songwriter and record producer who earns passive income from her music catalog, streaming services, merchandise, and endorsements.

Tips and steps for diversifying and expanding your income streams and sources.

Diversifying and expanding your income streams and sources may seem daunting or overwhelming, but it is not impossible or difficult. You can follow some tips and steps to make the process easier and smoother, such as:

Identifying and validating your income ideas and opportunities: Before you create and launch your income streams and sources, you need to identify and validate your income ideas and opportunities. You need to find out what your audience, followers, or customers want, need, or desire, and what they are willing to pay for. You can use various methods to identify and validate your income ideas and opportunities, such as:

Conduct market research, surveys, polls, or interviews, to gather data and feedback from your target market, niche, or audience.

Testing and experimenting with different income models, strategies, or platforms, to see what works and what doesn't, and to measure and analyze your results and performance.

Creating and offering minimum viable products (MVPs), prototypes, or samples, to gauge the demand and interest for your products or services, and to collect testimonials, reviews, or referrals.

Creating and launching your income offers and campaigns: After you identify and validate your income ideas and opportunities, you need to create and launch your income offers and campaigns. You need to design and develop your products or services and set up your income systems and processes. You also need to plan and execute your income launches and campaigns and generate awareness, attention, and excitement for your income offers. You can use various methods to create and launch your income offers and campaigns, such as:

Using tools, software, or resources, to create and deliver your products or services, such as e-book creators, course platforms, coaching platforms, etc.
Using tools, software, or resources, to set up and manage your income systems and processes, such as payment processors, invoicing systems, affiliate networks, etc.
Using tools, software, or resources, to plan and execute your income launches and campaigns, such as landing pages, email marketing, webinars, etc.

Marketing and delivering your income products or services: After you create and launch your income offers and campaigns, you need to market and deliver your income products or services. You need to attract and convert your prospects and leads and provide value, benefit, or solutions to your customers or clients. You also need to retain and nurture your customers or clients, and encourage repeat purchases, upsells, or cross-sells. You can use various methods to market and deliver your income products or services, such as:

Using your Twitter account, to share and distribute your income offers and campaigns, and to drive traffic and conversions to your income products or services.
Using your Twitter account, to provide customer service, feedback, or support, and to build trust, loyalty, or referrals for your income products or services.
Using your Twitter account, to create and share valuable content, such as tips, tricks, hacks, or insights, that can showcase and demonstrate your income products or services.

Managing and optimizing your income streams and sources: After you market and deliver your income products or services, you need to manage and optimize your income streams and sources. You need to monitor and track your income performance and results and identify and resolve any issues or problems. You also need to improve and enhance your income quality and quantity, and seek and implement any opportunities or suggestions. You can use various methods to manage and optimize your income streams and sources, such as:

Use tools, software, or resources, to monitor and track your income performance and results, such as analytics, dashboards, reports, etc.

Using tools, software, or resources, to identify and resolve any issues or problems, such as feedback, reviews, complaints, etc.

Using tools, software, or resources, to improve and enhance your income quality and quantity, such as testing, optimization, automation, etc.

Setting and tracking your goals and milestones and celebrating your achievements.

As a Twitter income earner, you have the opportunity to create value and impact with your content, products, and services. However, to succeed in this endeavor, you need to have a clear vision of what you want to achieve and how you will get there. This is where setting and tracking your goals and milestones comes in handy. We will discuss the importance and benefits of this practice, provide some examples and templates of SMART goals and milestones, suggest some tips and tools for setting and tracking them, and finally, discuss the importance and benefits of celebrating your achievements.

Why set and track your goals and milestones?

Setting and tracking your goals and milestones is a crucial habit for any Twitter income earner. Here are some of the reasons why:

It helps you clarify your purpose and direction. By setting and tracking your goals and milestones, you can define what you want to achieve, why you want to achieve it, and how you will measure your progress and success. This will support you in maintaining focus and motivation on your way.

It helps you plan your actions and strategies. By setting and tracking your goals and milestones, you can break down your big goals into smaller and manageable milestones, and identify the steps and resources you need to accomplish them. This will help you organize your time and energy, and avoid procrastination and overwhelm.

It helps you monitor your performance and results. By setting and tracking your goals and milestones, you can track your data and feedback, and evaluate your outcomes and impact. This will help you see what is working and what is not, and adjust your actions and strategies accordingly.

It helps you improve your skills and knowledge. By setting and tracking your goals and milestones, you can learn from your achievements and challenges, and identify your strengths and weaknesses. This will help you develop your competencies and expertise, and grow as a Twitter income earner.

How to set and track SMART goals and milestones.

One of the most effective ways to set and track your goals and milestones is to use the SMART criteria. SMART stands for Specific, Measurable, Achievable, Relevant, and Time-bound. A SMART goal or milestone is:

Specific: It clearly states what you want to achieve, and how you will achieve it. It addresses the questions of who, what, where, when, why, and how.

Measurable: It quantifies your desired outcome, and how you will track your progress and success. It addresses the question of how much, how many, or how often.

Achievable: It is realistic and attainable, given your current situation and resources. It answers the question of how possible or feasible it is.

Relevant: It aligns with your purpose and direction and contributes to your overall goal. It answers the question of how important or meaningful it is.

Time-bound: It has a specific deadline or timeframe, and creates a sense of urgency and accountability. It answers the question of when or how soon.

Here are some examples and templates of SMART goals and milestones that you can set and track as a Twitter income earner:

Increasing your Twitter followers by X% in Y months: This is a SMART goal that can help you grow your audience and reach on Twitter. To achieve this goal, you can set and track SMART milestones, such as:

Posting X number of tweets per week that are relevant, engaging, and valuable to your target audience.
Use X number of hashtags per tweet that are popular, relevant, and specific to your niche.
Following X number of accounts per week that are related to your niche, and interacting with their tweets.
Joining X number of Twitter chats or spaces per month that are relevant to your niche, and sharing your insights and opinions.
Creating X number of polls, quizzes, or giveaways per month that are fun, interactive, and rewarding to your followers.

Earning $X from Twitter income in Y months: This is a SMART goal that can help you monetize your content, products, and services on Twitter. To achieve this goal, you can set and track SMART milestones, such as:
Creating X number of products or services per month that are valuable, unique, and relevant to your niche and audience.

Launching X number of marketing campaigns per month that are creative, persuasive, and effective to promote your products or services.

Generating X number of leads or prospects per month that are interested, qualified, and ready to buy your products or services.

Converting X number of leads or prospects into customers or clients per month that are satisfied, loyal, and profitable.

Retaining X number of customers or clients per month that are repeat, referral, or testimonial sources.

Launching your new product or service in Y months: This is a SMART goal that can help you create and deliver value and impact with your new product or service. To achieve this goal, you can set and track SMART milestones, such as:

Conducting X number of market research or customer interviews per month to identify the needs, problems, and desires of your target audience.

Developing X number of prototypes or mockups per month to test and validate your product or service idea and features.

Soliciting X number of feedback or reviews per month to improve and refine your product or service quality and usability.

Building X number of partnerships or collaborations per month to leverage your network and resources, and increase your exposure and credibility.

Preparing X number of launch materials or assets per month to generate buzz and excitement, and attract and convert your potential customers or clients.

Reaching X number of downloads, views, subscribers, etc. in Y months: This is a SMART goal that can help you measure and demonstrate your value and impact with your content, products, and services. To achieve this goal, you can set and track SMART milestones, such as:

Creating X number of content pieces per month that are informative, entertaining, and inspiring to your target audience.

Optimizing X number of content pieces per month for SEO, keywords, and hashtags to increase your visibility and discoverability.

Distributing X number of content pieces per month across different platforms, channels, and formats to expand your reach and engagement.

Repurposing X number of content pieces per month into different types, such as blog posts, podcasts, videos, ebooks, etc. to diversify your content and audience.

Analyzing X number of content pieces per month for performance, results, and feedback to optimize your content and strategy.

What are some tips and tools for setting and tracking your goals and milestones?

Setting and tracking your goals and milestones can be challenging and overwhelming, especially if you have multiple or complex goals and milestones. Here are some tips and tools that can help you with this process:

Breaking down your big goals into smaller and manageable milestones: This can help you simplify your goals and milestones, and make them more achievable and actionable. You can use the SMART criteria to break down your big goals into smaller and manageable milestones and assign them to specific periods, such as daily, weekly, monthly, quarterly, etc.

Use tools and apps, such as Trello, Asana, Google Sheets, etc. to plan and monitor your progress: This can help you organize and visualize your goals and milestones, and track your data and feedback. You can use tools and apps, such as Trello, Asana,

Google Sheets, etc. to create and manage your goal and milestone boards, lists, charts, etc., and update them regularly with your progress and results.

Reviewing and adjusting your goals and milestones regularly: This can help you evaluate and improve your goals and milestones, and adapt to changing situations and circumstances. You can review and adjust your goals and milestones regularly, such as weekly, monthly, quarterly, etc. based on your data and feedback, and make necessary changes or corrections to your actions and strategies.

Seeking and receiving feedback and support from others: This can help you enhance and validate your goals and milestones, and overcome challenges and difficulties. You can seek and receive feedback and support from others, such as mentors, coaches, peers, friends, family, etc. who can offer you guidance, advice, encouragement, accountability, etc.

Why celebrate your achievements?

Setting and tracking your goals and milestones is not enough. You also need to celebrate your achievements, no matter how big or small they are. Celebrating your achievements is important and beneficial for several reasons:

It boosts your confidence and self-esteem. By celebrating your achievements, you can acknowledge and appreciate your efforts and results, and recognize your value and worth. This can boost your confidence and self-esteem, and make you feel proud and happy about yourself and your work.

It enhances your motivation and enthusiasm. By celebrating your achievements, you can reward and reinforce your positive behaviors and outcomes, and create a positive feedback loop. This can enhance your motivation and enthusiasm, and make you eager and excited to pursue your next goals and milestones.

It strengthens your relationships and connections. By celebrating your achievements, you can share and celebrate your achievements with your Twitter followers and other supporters, and express your gratitude and appreciation to them. This can strengthen your relationships and connections, and make you feel supported and valued by others.

It improves your well-being and happiness. By celebrating your achievements, you can enjoy and savor your achievements, and experience positive emotions and feelings, such as joy, satisfaction, gratitude, etc.

How to celebrate your achievements.

There are many ways to celebrate your achievements as a Twitter income earner. Here are some examples and ideas of how to do so:

Sharing and celebrating your achievements with your Twitter followers and other supporters: This can help you spread and amplify your achievements, and inspire and influence others. You can share and celebrate your achievements with your Twitter followers and other supporters by:
Posting tweets or threads that showcase your achievements, such as screenshots, testimonials, reviews, etc.
Creating content that highlights your achievements, such as blog posts, podcasts, videos, ebooks, etc.
Hosting events that celebrate your achievements, such as webinars, workshops, Q&A sessions, etc.

Inviting your followers and supporters to join your celebrations, such as by commenting, liking, retweeting, sharing, etc.

Rewarding yourself with something that you enjoy or value, such as a treat, a gift, a vacation, etc: This can help you relax and recharge, and enjoy the fruits of your labor. You can reward yourself with something that you enjoy or value, such as a treat, a gift, a vacation, etc. by:
Treat yourself to something that you love or crave, such as a meal, a drink, a dessert, etc.
Buying yourself something that you want or need, such as a gadget, a book, a course, etc.
Take yourself to somewhere that you like or dream of, such as a park, a beach, a city, etc.
Giving yourself some time off or a break from your work, such as a day, a week, a month, etc.

Reflecting and learning from your achievements and challenges: This can help you grow and improve, and prepare for your next goals and milestones. You can reflect and learn from your achievements and challenges by:
Writing down or journaling your achievements and challenges, and what you learned from them.
Reviewing or revisiting your goals and milestones, and how you achieved them.
Identifying or listing your strengths and weaknesses, and how you can leverage or improve them.
Setting or updating your new goals and milestones, and how you will pursue them.

Expressing gratitude and appreciation to yourself and others who helped you along the way: This can help you cultivate and maintain a positive and grateful mindset, and strengthen your relationships and connections. You can express gratitude and appreciation to yourself and others who helped you along the way by:

Saying or writing thank you notes or messages to yourself and others who helped you along the way

Giving or sending gifts or tokens of appreciation to yourself and others who helped you along the way

Praising or complimenting yourself and others who helped you along the way

Recommending or endorsing yourself and others who helped you along the way.

Continuously learning and improving your skills and knowledge in Twitter income generation.

Twitter is a highly competitive and dynamic environment, where trends, algorithms, and user preferences change constantly. To succeed and thrive in Twitter income generation, you need to continuously learn and improve your skills and knowledge in this field. This will help you to:

Stay updated and relevant in your niche or industry.
Adapt and optimize your strategies and tactics.
Enhance and diversify your income streams.
Grow and engage your audience and network.
Increase your credibility and authority.
Avoid or overcome common challenges and pitfalls.

There are many ways to learn and improve your skills and knowledge in Twitter income generation, depending on your goals, needs, and preferences. Some of the most common and effective methods are:

Reading and following the latest trends, news, and updates on Twitter and Twitter income: You can use tools like Twitter Trends, Twitter Moments, Twitter Analytics, and Twitter Lists to discover and monitor what is happening and popular on the platform. You can also follow and learn from successful and influential Twitter users, experts, and mentors in your niche or industry, and see how they generate income from their tweets.

Taking and completing online courses, webinars, workshops, etc. on Twitter and Twitter income: There are many online learning platforms and resources that offer comprehensive and practical courses on various aspects of Twitter income generation, such as

Twitter Marketing, Twitter Ads, Twitter Affiliate Marketing, Twitter Influencer Marketing, Twitter Content Creation, etc. You can choose the ones that suit your level, budget, and schedule, and learn from the best practices and tips of the instructors and peers.

Reading and studying books, articles, blogs, podcasts, etc. on Twitter and Twitter income: There are also many books, articles, blogs, podcasts, and other media that provide valuable and insightful information and advice on Twitter income generation. You can read and study them at your own pace and convenience, and gain deeper and broader knowledge and understanding of the topic. Some of the recommended books, articles, blogs, and podcasts are:

Twitter Money Master: A book by Nick Tsai that teaches you how to make money on Twitter with proven and easy-to-follow strategies.

How to Make Money on Twitter: 15 Ways to Earn Income: An article by Adam Enfroy that explains 15 different ways to earn income on Twitter, with examples and steps.

Twitter Marketing Blog: A blog by Twitter that shares the latest news, insights, and best practices on how to use Twitter for marketing and business purposes.

The Twitter Smarter Podcast: A podcast by Madalyn Sklar that features interviews with Twitter experts and influencers who share their secrets and tips on how to grow your Twitter presence and income.

Practicing and applying your skills and knowledge in Twitter income generation: The best way to learn and improve your skills and knowledge in Twitter income generation is to practice and apply them in real situations. You can start by setting realistic and measurable goals and objectives for your Twitter income generation, such as:

How much income do you want to generate from Twitter?
What are the sources and methods of your Twitter income generation?
Who are your target audience and customers on Twitter?
What are the value propositions and benefits of your Twitter income generation?
How will you measure and evaluate your Twitter income generation performance and results?

Then, you can implement and execute your Twitter income generation plan, using the skills and knowledge that you have learned and acquired. You can also monitor and track your progress and outcomes, and make adjustments and improvements as needed.

To continuously learn and improve your skills and knowledge in Twitter income generation, you also need to develop some habits and tips that will help you to stay motivated and focused, such as:

Setting aside time and budget for your learning and improvement activities: You should allocate a specific amount of time and money for your learning and improvement activities, and stick to it. This will help you to prioritize and commit to your learning and improvement goals, and avoid distractions and procrastination. You can also use tools like calendars, reminders, timers, and planners to organize and manage your learning and improvement schedule and budget.

Choosing and focusing on the skills and knowledge that are most relevant and useful for your Twitter income goals and needs: You should not try to learn and improve everything at once, as this will overwhelm and confuse you. Instead, you should identify and focus on the skills and knowledge that are most relevant and useful for your Twitter income generation, and that will give you the most return on your investment. You can use tools like SWOT analysis, gap analysis, and feedback surveys to assess and determine your strengths, weaknesses, opportunities, and threats in Twitter income generation, and to find out the areas that need improvement and enhancement.

Seeking and applying feedback and suggestions from others: You should not learn and improve your skills and knowledge in Twitter income generation in isolation. You should seek and apply feedback and suggestions from others, such as your audience, customers, partners, mentors, peers, and experts. This will help you to gain new perspectives and insights, to discover and correct your mistakes and errors, to learn from the experiences and lessons of others, and to improve your performance and results. You can use tools like surveys, polls, reviews, ratings, comments, and testimonials to collect and analyze feedback and suggestions from others, and to implement and incorporate them into your Twitter income generation plan and actions.

Experimenting and testing new ideas and methods: You should not be afraid or reluctant to experiment and test new ideas and methods in Twitter income generation. You should be open and curious to try new things and explore new possibilities, as this will help you to learn and improve your skills and knowledge, find out what works and what does not, innovate and differentiate yourself from the competition, and increase your chances of success and growth. You can use tools like A/B testing, split testing, and multivariate testing to experiment and test new ideas and methods in Twitter income generation, and to compare and evaluate their effectiveness and efficiency.

Twitter income generation is a rewarding and exciting opportunity for anyone who wants to make money online. However, it is also a challenging and demanding endeavor that requires continuous learning and improvement of your skills and knowledge. By following the methods, habits, and tips discussed above, you can learn and improve your skills and knowledge in Twitter income generation, and achieve your Twitter income goals and dreams.

In this chapter, we have explored some innovative tips for success in generating income from Twitter. We have learned how to:

Experiment and test new features, formats, and strategies to optimize your Twitter income. By trying out different approaches, you can discover what works best for your audience, niche, and goals. You can also take advantage of the latest trends and opportunities on Twitter to boost your visibility and engagement.

Leverage tools and resources that can help you automate, streamline, and enhance your Twitter income activities. By using various tools and resources, you can save time, money, and effort in managing your Twitter account, creating and sharing content, and monetizing your tweets. You can also improve the quality and performance of your Twitter income activities by using analytics, feedback, and insights.

Collaborate and network with other Twitter users, influencers, and experts to learn, exchange, and support each other. By building relationships and connections on Twitter, you can expand your reach, influence, and credibility. You can also learn from the best practices and experiences of others, exchange ideas and opportunities, and support each other in achieving your Twitter income goals.

Diversify and expand your income streams and sources to increase your earning potential and reduce your risks. By creating multiple income streams and sources from Twitter, you can maximize your income potential and minimize your dependence on any single source. You can also explore new and creative ways to monetize your Twitter presence and content.

Set and track your goals and milestones and celebrate your achievements. By setting and tracking your goals and milestones, you can measure your progress and success in generating income from Twitter. You can also identify your strengths and weaknesses, and adjust your strategies and actions accordingly. Moreover, by celebrating your achievements, you can motivate yourself and others, and appreciate your efforts and results.

Continuously learn and improve your skills and knowledge in Twitter income generation. By keeping yourself updated and informed about the latest developments and changes on Twitter, you can adapt and thrive in the dynamic and competitive Twitter income environment. You can also enhance your skills and knowledge by seeking feedback, guidance, and training from experts and mentors.

We hope that this chapter has provided you with some useful and practical tips for success in generating income from Twitter. By applying these tips, you can increase your chances of achieving your Twitter income goals and dreams. Remember, the key to success is to be consistent, creative, and committed in your Twitter income activities.

Conclusion

You have reached the end of this book, and I hope you have learned a lot from it. In this book, We have shared with you the secrets and strategies to make money on Twitter, one of the most popular and powerful social media platforms in the world.

Twitter is not only a place to share your thoughts, opinions, and stories, but also a platform to showcase your value, build your brand, and generate income. Whether you are an individual, a business, or an organization, you can use Twitter to reach and engage with your target audience and offer them solutions, products, or services that they need or want.

In this book, we have covered the following topics:

How to build a strategic and attractive Twitter account that reflects your brand and personality, and attracts and retains your followers

How to create and share valuable and relevant content that solves problems, educates, entertains, or inspires your followers, and increases your engagement and influence

How to optimize your impressions by using hashtags, keywords, and trending topics naturally and strategically, and joining or creating hashtag campaigns, challenges, and movements

How to explore and evaluate the various income opportunities and models available on Twitter, and find and partner with brands, businesses, and platforms that offer paid opportunities for Twitter users

How to sell your products and services, become an affiliate marketer, launch creator subscriptions, or join the X Ads Revenue Sharing Program, and earn money from your tweets and bio

How to avoid common mistakes and pitfalls when making money on Twitter, such as violating Twitter rules and policies, annoying or alienating your followers, compromising your reputation and credibility, or handling negative feedback poorly
How to experiment and test new features, formats, and strategies, leverage tools and resources, collaborate and network with other Twitter users, diversify and expand your income streams and sources, and set and achieve your Twitter income goals

By applying the tips and techniques that we have shared with you in this book, you will be able to turn your Twitter account into a money-making machine and enjoy the benefits of having an additional or alternative source of income.

However, making money on Twitter is not a get-rich-quick scheme, nor a one-size-fits-all solution. It requires time, effort, patience, and persistence. It also requires creativity, innovation, and adaptation. You need to be willing to learn, experiment, and improve, and to keep up with the ever-changing and evolving Twitter income landscape.

I hope this book has inspired and motivated you to take action and start making money on Twitter. I also hope this book has provided you with the information and guidance you need to succeed in your Twitter income journey.

Thank you for reading this book, and I wish you all the best in your Twitter income endeavors. If you have any questions, feedback, or suggestions, please feel free to contact me at Biceglobal@gmail.com. I would love to hear from you and help you in any way I can.

Happy tweeting and earning!